SUMMUM®

SEALED EXCEPT TO THE OPEN MIND

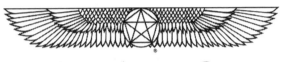

SYMBOL OF RA

SUMMUM®

SEALED EXCEPT TO THE OPEN MIND

Summum Bonum Amen Ra

~ 2nd Edition ~

Summum
Salt Lake City, Utah

Summum
707 Genesee Avenue
Salt Lake City, Utah 84104
www.summum.us

Published February 2020

1st edition published 1988
2nd edition 2020

ISBN: 978-0-943217-14-7 (paperback)
ISBN: 978-0-943217-15-4 (hardcover)
ISBN: 978-0-943217-16-1 (epub)

Library of Congress Control Number: 2019921023

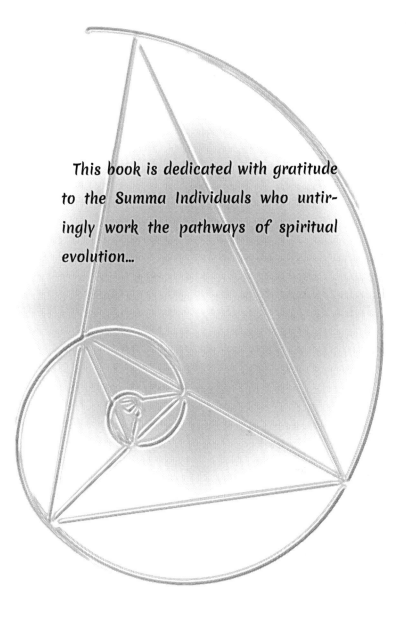

This book is dedicated with gratitude to the Summa Individuals who untiringly work the pathways of spiritual evolution...

Does anyone have a definition of philosophy? I got one out of the dictionary. I'll read it to you. It says, "Love of, or search for wisdom and knowledge; theory of logical analysis of the principles underlying conduct, thought, knowledge, and the nature of the universe."

Does that pretty well describe what we do around here?

— AMEN RA

CONTENTS

ACKNOWLEDGEMENTS

With special appreciation I would like to gratefully acknowledge the helpful assistance of Anu Aua for his help in the editing and structure of this work. I would also like to thank Anu Aua for making this information available online in this age of Internet technology.

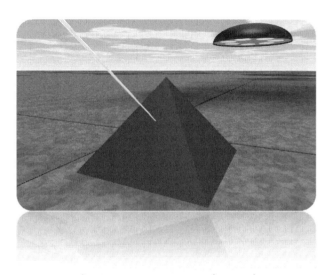

They're assistants on the path of evolution, and that's their whole purpose, to assist souls through evolution. They work with lots of people... in different states of evolution. In "The Egyptian Book of the Dead," they call them door keepers or gate keepers. They are simply individuals who help others – guides helping others in evolution. They don't speak with their mouths, they speak with telepathy. It's in concepts versus words.

— AMEN RA

INTRODUCTION

1 "When the student's mind is open, then comes the voice to fill it with wisdom." — Summum

2 This book is dedicated with gratitude to the Summa Individuals who untiringly work the pathways of spiritual evolution, and who with great concern have presented to me these principles. These teachings cannot be accredited to any one person or human source, for these teachings represent the workings of Creation Itself. These principles have been presented previously to those souls evolved enough to understand them, and again the nature of Creation is presented to those now ready.

3 The purpose of this work is to allow those searching for a comprehension of Creation to receive the keys to that understanding; to use these keys to unlock the many facets, and to reconcile the many bits of knowledge they may have acquired but which have not satisfied their understanding of the whole. Those advanced on the path will

find this book to be a master key which may open the many esoteric doors to Creation.

4   These teachings are not occult. These concepts have always existed, and as an eternal work are presented by advanced Summa Individuals to those searching for the source of Creation. The Summa Individuals come attired in nothing but their naked, innocent form with words most appropriate for every age in which they bring the teachings. Recorded history is replete with masters, Adam, Moses, Krishna, Buddha, Christ, and Mohammed having been taught by the angelic beings. Even today the Summa Individuals continue to present the principles.

5   The basic knowledge of these principles forms the esoteric teachings of every race and religion. Even the most ancient teachings of India and Egypt have their roots in these principles. Advanced masters from all areas of this planet have been taught and enlightened throughout time by the Summa Individuals — beings who come to this planet to assist those searching for the tools to unlock the mysteries of Creation. It is from these evolved entities (the continuum), that the master key has been obtained.

6   These principles are the basic underlying foundation of all existence, forming the basis for all displayed phenomena. Just as all music is an orchestration of the fundamental tones of a musical scale, all material existence is an orchestration of the principles. Just as all color is a combination and expression of the primary colors, all existence is a combination and expression of the principles.

7   The principles within this book are so powerful that despite the many different teachings which have evolved, there may still be found certain basic similarities between

the many religious theories entertained today. The student of comparative religion will be able to perceive the influence of the Eternal Principles in every known religion, whether it be a dead religion or a living one.

8   These principles are the essence which has blossomed in many different forms, rather than establishing a single discipline of philosophy which would dominate the world's thought. Nevertheless, these principles have been restored to their purity by the Summa Individuals at this time. Naturally, undeveloped students will not comprehend these principles, for they are reserved for the few who are ready to master them.

9   Once again, there are a few individuals who are being initiated into the mysteries of these principles by advanced beings, for the purity of the teachings has degenerated. That is why so many people are so uncomfortable with the current forms of religious practice. These initiates may not receive popular approval. Yet they are indifferent to these conditions for they know how few in each generation are ready for this knowledge. These pearls of wisdom are for the few who recognize their value and hold them deep in their souls as vehicles of spiritual progression.

10   Regarding the transmission of the master key to those ready to receive it, it has been said: "Where is heard the voice of the Master, the open mind of those ready for the teaching listens." But the teacher's customary attitude has always been strictly in accordance with another principle: "The voice of wisdom is silent, except to the open mind."

11   Contrary to popular opinion, these initiates have never sought to become martyrs. However, there are certain principles which, when publicly promulgated, bring great

cries of scorn and persecution from the so called "religious." Yet a few are capable of understanding the principles and have advanced along the path with the teacher.

12   In this work, the Master Key as taught by the Summa Individuals is given to you. These are fundamental Principles of Creation. These are the working principles, and it is left to you to apply these principles for yourself. There will be those who read this book who will refuse to understand how Creation provides for the continuance of the work, which must recreate itself in every age. Sometimes the work is neglected but it cannot remain so forever. The master key which unlocks the Principles of Creation is a constant. However, the application is best adapted from age to age.[1]

13   If you are truly searching for the keys to Creation, you will be able to resolve and apply these principles. If not, then you must develop yourself in other ways, for these principles will be nothing more than "words, words, words" to you.

(A<small>MAN</small>)

S<small>UMMUM</small> B<small>ONUM</small> (A<small>MEN</small>) R<small>A</small>

(A<small>MIN</small>)

(A<small>MON</small>)

(A<small>MUN</small>)

---

[1] Throughout history, countless writings have referenced the Principles of Creation in one way or another. The majority of writings indirectly reference the principles, giving only hints that may allude to their existence. Few are direct and explicit. Over time, the information tends to become fragmented or distorted and incomplete, but eventually it is re-compiled and returned to a pure, fundamental form. In addition, styles, languages, and methods of communication continue to evolve. Therefore, explanations of the principles must be re-written and adapted for each age in order to present them in a form more easily understood by the people of that era. That is what this work represents.

A university study found that people only see and understand those things that are part of their environmental system or their belief system. So you may not see or realize something right before you because of your mental conditioning. You need to build an appropriate environmental system to be able to recognize things, understand them, become aware of them, or know what they're about. We call this the Systematic Law of Learning.

— AMEN RA

CHAPTER 1

THE SUMMUM PHILOSOPHY

1   "The voice of wisdom is silent, except to the OPEN MIND." — Summum

2   The Summum philosophy embodies the Principles of Creation Itself. From Grand Cycle to Grand Cycle the fundamental esoteric teachings of the Summum Bonum are taught to select advanced souls who then progress to new spiritual levels. The last recorded reservoir of these teachings on planet Earth has been found in Egypt, a home of the pyramids. All nations have borrowed from the ancient inheritance of Egypt. India, Persia, China, Japan, ancient Greece, Rome, and other countries partook liberally at the feast of knowledge which the masters of the land of Ra and Isis so freely provided for them.

3   At the ascension of the Grand Cycles, the Summa Individuals enlighten the souls and minds of those ready to receive the knowledge. These Summa Individuals are referred to as the "Neters" in the ancient Egyptian hiero-

glyphs. Here on planet Earth, the pyramids were used as the storage house from which knowledge stored potentially could be obtained, transmitted, and then used dynamically to catapult the select advanced souls forward in evolution. Within the pyramid sanctuaries the student would enter, then emerge as initiate or master to travel the four corners of the Earth carrying with them the precious kinetic knowledge. All serious students of these principles recognize the debt they owe to these venerable masters of those ancient lands and to their teachers, the Summa Individuals.

4   Even the teachings of the Gnostic and Early Christians drew their roots from the Summum principles. Unfortunately, these same teachings were lost at the time of Constantine whose iron hand smothered philosophy with its blanket of theology. The loss to the Christian Church was incalculable, for its very essence and spirit was gutted. Its participants were thrown into the abyss of the dark ages.

5   The restored purity of these principles rests with the faithful souls who dedicate their lives to keep alive the message of these teachings. These teachings are not found in books to any great extent. The understanding is passed on from master to initiate; from initiate to student; from voice to open mind. Even today there will be found but few reliable books on this philosophy, although there are countless references to it in various phases of science, metaphysics, religion, and philosophy. Yet the Summum principles are the only master key which will open all doors to the knowledge of Creation!

6   These principles are formulated through nature and cannot be ascribed to a god or humankind. It is these prin-

ciples which are the cause of "gods" and humankind, not vice versa. It is not possible to understand these principles using the intellect alone, for they must be experienced; and humankind, through its experience, must evolve to this understanding. The Law of Knowledge must be applied to all principles for one to have real knowledge rather than just belief. This systematic law of learning requires you to first question the principle and read the "words" about it. Secondly, you must take activity in the principle and experience the action, the "cause and effect" of the principle. Thirdly, you move to a knowledge of, rather than a belief about the principle, for the principle and its workings become your personal knowledge through experience.

7   For example, let us suppose you have never eaten an almond before and you would like me to convey to you the knowledge of what an almond tastes like. I can tell you that an almond tastes sweet, that it is crunchy, bitter, smooth, or dry, and describe it in other ways. You now have a description about what an almond tastes like. At this point you still do not know what an almond tastes like because all you have is some sort of belief of what it tastes like based upon my description of it. There really is no description that can convey to you what an almond tastes like. The only way you are going to know for yourself, rather than just having a belief, is for you to experience the taste of an almond through your personal experience of eating an almond. A knowledge of the Principles of Summum requires you to apply the systematic law of learning and experience them, or they will be as mere "words, words, words" to you.

8   There have been collections of maxims, axioms, aphorisms, and precepts which are mostly not understandable
to outsiders, but which are readily understood by the initiate once explained and exemplified by the masters. These
teachings really constitute the basic principles of Psychokinesis which, contrary to the general belief, deals with
the mastery of mental forces rather than material elements.
Psychokinesis is really the alteration of one kind of mental
vibration into another, a much more encompassing, varied,
and dynamic process. The alteration of material forms
(such as the changing of one kind of metal into another) is
but an aspect of psychokinesis.

9   **"Where is heard the voice of the Master, the mind
of those ready for the teaching is open." — Summum**

10   **"When the student's mind is open, then comes the
voice to fill it with wisdom." — Summum**

11   According to these aphorisms, this book will attract the
attention of those prepared to receive the teaching. Likewise, when the pupil is ready to receive the wisdom, then
will this little book come to him or her. Such is the law.
The Principle of Cause and Effect, in its aspect of the Law
of Attraction, will bring the voice and open mind together.
The student and this book thus come together.

12   Since this book has come into your hands, you are now
at a point in life to be exposed to the Summum philosophy.

When you first hear this explanation of where God and everything came from, you may not understand it. But after continued examination, it starts to make sense. Allow yourself to be open to it and allow it to be within you. The more you consider and study it, all of a sudden it talks back to you. It starts to sing a song to you telling why it is, what it is, and how it is.

— AMEN RA

CHAPTER 2

CREATION

1   "NOTHING AND POSSIBILITY come in and out of bond infinite times in a finite moment." — Summum

2   Aeons ago, the material universe and everything within it exploded into being. The creation of the material universe is the single known paramount event from which all other known events precipitate. That it happened is obvious. Why it happened is the greatest mystery you have ever known. The enigma surrounding the cause of existence has forever captivated humankind's thought, and you search for the answer to this mystery in the questions, "Who am I?" "Why am I here?" "How did the universe come into being?" "Where did God come from?"

3   The Grand Principle of Creation is presented here for your examination. It is the answer to the greatest mysteries which dwell within the thinking human mind. No record of this principle may be found anywhere except within this

book. With diligence and openness, study, learn, and apply the principles and techniques presented in this work. As you progress, you will gain an understanding and come to know the Grand Principle of Creation.

4   Before the material universe manifested there was NO THING. If there was NO THING (NOTHING), then it must have been possible for nothing to be. If it is possible for NO THING to be, then it must be possible for everything to be — all matter, "space-time," all relativity — all this must be possible. If there is All Possibility, then there must be the possibility of the NO THING (NOTHING). In the same fashion it must be possible for ALL THINGS to be (SUMMUM). Automatically, with no beginning and no end, do these Grand Opposites "come in and out of bond infinite times in a finite moment" — therefore creating a series of infinite "EVENTS." These infinite EVENTS, held within the finite moment of singularity, manifest as infinite conceptualized energy that is then externalized through phenomenal, inconceivable projections, limitless in number. Among these countless projections, one produced your universe through an extreme rapid expansion, what has been called the BIG BANG — an EVENT. In essence, there are infinite "Big Bangs" creating infinite universes whose origin is an eternal, finite moment of infinite EVENTS, all produced by NOTHING and POSSIBILITY.

5   A corollary to this Grand Principle is, "It is impossible for two things to join in harmony or discord without the presence of a third, for a 'BOND' must exist to unite them" — the copulation generates SUMMUM. It is the BONDing of NOTHING and POSSIBILITY infinite times within this finite moment which is the birth of the cosmos and all sub-

sequent EVENTS. "It takes the joining of TWO to make one — SUMMUM."

6   Although your physicists and astronomers have determined the origin of the material universe, they are incapable of determining the MOMENT just prior to the BIG BANG. This cannot be examined by formulas, because formulas use the methodology of the material universe. Just prior to the EVENT (singularity), "space-time" and therefore "matter" did not exist, so it is impossible to make formulations based upon the non-reality of these systems. To be totally correct one would have to say there was no MOMENT just prior to the BIG BANG, for time did not exist. So when physicists try to examine the origin of the Creation, they must be confined to studying philosophical states, and they are not comfortable doing this at this time.

7   Physicists who deal in quantum mechanics state: "You cannot (objectively) observe something without changing it in the process." This statement is based upon what is termed the Uncertainty Principle, which means that when you observe one aspect of a thing (such as an electron), you are forever uncertain of any other aspects of that same thing.[1] Consequently, they are restricted to using collections of probabilities in describing the motion of things. Further, they state that the existence of the collection of probabilities establishes what would happen if an observation occurred. (Note that the term PROBABILITIES is closely related to the term POSSIBILITIES). To the extent that the Uncertainty Principle is applied to the origin of the universe, you can readily understand the problem with the physicists' objective measurements (observations). No objective measurements are possible in solving this problem.

8   The Grand Principle of Creation embodies your SUB-JECTIVE OBSERVATION of Creation Itself, in which the process of OBSERVATION between NOTHING and POS-SIBILITY produces the EVENT of Creation. This condition, in which the two grand opposites are poised in opposition to one another, results in SUMMUM: the sum total of everything. When one state of being observes another, there is created an automatic connection between the two. It is this relationship between POSSIBILITY and NOTHING which generates this incredible EVENT. The EVENT includes all outward manifestations and appearances which you know under the terms of "the material universe," "the phenomena of life," "matter," "energy," "space-time," "distance," "speed," "relativity," and, in short, all that is apparent to your material senses.

9   SUMMUM, created by the copulation of NOTHING and POSSIBILITY, is SPIRIT, and may be considered and thought of as A UNIVERSAL, INFINITE, LIVING MIND. This MIND is the effect of CREATION'S "copulation," manifesting the qualities of nothingness and (SUMMUM) possibility. From the copulation of CREATION emanate the seven Great Principles of Summum: PSYCHOKINESIS, CORRESPONDENCE,   VIBRATION,   OPPOSITION, RHYTHM, CAUSE AND EFFECT, and GENDER. These principles are the NATURE of the Grand Copulation of CREATION.

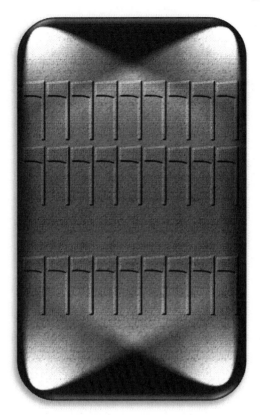

---

[1] Despite the Uncertainty Principle's significant role in Quantum Mechanics, it can only be considered partially true due to the effect of paradox. The Divine Paradox which is discussed later in this work reveals that all truths are only partially true and must be applied in the examination of anything. The Einstein-Podolsky-Rosen thought experiment demonstrates the ability to know more information about a system than the Uncertainty Principle would allow, hence the infamous EPR paradox. The demonstration of teleportation through Entanglement which utilizes EPR beams to transport quantum states from one point to another exploits the restrictions of Uncertainty. Yet regardless of the methods scientists use to examine the universe, as long as they confine themselves to objective measurements (observation), the mystery of Creation will always remain elusive.

If you look at the principles and all the events in your life and you apply them, it answers all the questions. It reconciles everything. It brings a comfort and a peace into your life that allows things to be.

— AMEN RA

CHAPTER 3

SEVEN SUMMUM PRINCIPLES

1   "The Principles of knowing Creation are seven;
those who know these possess the Magic Key to
whose touch all locked doors open to Creation."
— Summum

2   The seven great Summum principles upon which the
Summum philosophy is based are as follows:

   I. THE PRINCIPLE OF PSYCHOKINESIS

   II. THE PRINCIPLE OF CORRESPONDENCE

   III. THE PRINCIPLE OF VIBRATION

   IV. THE PRINCIPLE OF OPPOSITION

   V. THE PRINCIPLE OF RHYTHM

   VI. THE PRINCIPLE OF CAUSE & EFFECT

   VII. THE PRINCIPLE OF GENDER

3　These seven great principles will be discussed and explained at length in this work. A short explanation of each, however, will be given at this point, for all the Principles of Summum have an interrelationship with each other.

I. THE PRINCIPLE OF PSYCHOKINESIS

4　*"SUMMUM is MIND; the universe is a mental creation."* — Summum

5　This first great principle embodies the idea that "All is Mind." It explains that SUMMUM (which is the substantial essence underlying all the outward manifestations and appearances which you know under the terms of "the material universe," "the phenomena of life," "matter," "energy," "space-time," "distance," "speed," "relativity," and, in short, all that is apparent to your material senses) is SPIRIT. This SPIRIT may be considered and thought of as A UNIVERSAL, INFINITE, LIVING MIND.

6　This living MIND performs gastrulation, which is a turning of itself inside out, manifesting its esoteric NATURE outwardly. Therefore, all the phenomenal worlds and universes are simply a mental creation of SUMMUM (MIND), subject to the laws of created things; and the universes, as a whole and in their parts or units, have their existence in the Mind of SUMMUM. It is in this Mind that we "live and move and have our being." This SUBJECTIVE OBSERVATION of CREATION is the principle which establishes the mental nature of the universes and easily explains all of the varied mental and psychic phenomena.

Without such explanation these phenomena are not understandable and defy scientific inspection. An understanding
of this first great Principle of Psychokinesis empowers the
individual to comprehend the laws of the mental universe,
and to apply the same to his or her well-being and
RHYTHMED advancement. The serious student is empowered to apply intelligently the great mental laws, instead of using them in a haphazard manner. With the Master Key in his or her possession, the student may unlock
the many doors of the mental and psychic sanctuaries of
knowledge and enter the same freely and intelligently.
This principle explains the NATURE of matter, energy,
space-time, and why and how all these are subordinate to
the mastery of mind. Those who understand the
knowledge of the mental nature of the universe are well
advanced on the path to mastery. Without this master key,
mastery is impossible, and the student knocks in vain at
the many doors of Creation.

II. THE PRINCIPLE OF CORRESPONDENCE

7   *"As above, so below; as below, so above."* — Summum

8   This principle embodies the idea that there is always a
correspondence or correlation between the laws and phenomena of the various levels of being and life. This apho-
rism, "As above, so below; as below, so above," gives one
the means of solving many a mysterious paradox and hidden secrets of nature. There are levels beyond your knowing, but when you apply the Principle of Correspondence
to them you are able to understand much that would oth-

erwise be unknowable to you. This principle exists at the various levels of the material, mental, and spiritual universes and is of universal application. This principle has been considered to be one of the most important mental instruments by which humankind is able to set aside the obstacles which hide the unknown from view. Its use can even remove the "Veil of Isis" (death) so that one can catch a glimpse of the other side. Just as a knowledge of the principles of geometry empowers the astronomer to measure distant suns and their movements while seated in an observatory, a knowledge of the Principle of Correspondence empowers you to reason intelligently from the known to the unknown. All the Principles of Summum have an interrelationship with Correspondence. Correspondence draws its NATURE from the copulation of CREATION. Studying the monad, one is studying the universe.

III. THE PRINCIPLE OF VIBRATION

9   *"Nothing rests; everything moves; everything vibrates."*
— Summum

10   This principle embodies the idea that everything is in motion; everything vibrates; nothing is at rest; facts which science endorses and which each new scientific discovery tends to verify. Yet this principle was enunciated thousands of years ago by masters of old. This principle explains that the differences between various manifestations of matter, energy, space-time, mind, and even spirit result largely from varying rates of vibration. From CREATION's copulation (SUMMUM), which is pure spirit, down to the

grossest form of matter, all is in vibration. From the "in and out of bond infinite times in a finite moment" (CREATION's copulation), to the expansion and collapse of a universe, the rate of vibration is observed as states of "proper" time. The higher the vibration, the higher the position in the scale. The vibration of spirit is at such an infinite rate of intensity and rapidity that it is seemingly at rest — just as a rapidly turning wheel seems to be motionless. At the other end of the scale, there are gross forms of matter whose vibrations are so low as to seem at rest. Between these two opposing points, there are billions upon billions of varying degrees of vibration. From quark, squark, lepton, slepton, electron, atom, and molecule, to planets and universes, everything is in vibratory motion. This is also true in the fields of energy and force (which are but varying degrees of vibration); and also at the mental levels (whose states depend upon vibrations); and even at the spiritual levels. All the Principles of Summum have an interrelationship with Vibration. Vibration draws its NATURE from the copulation of CREATION. An understanding of the principle, with the appropriate application, empowers the student to control their own mental vibrations as well as those of others. The masters also apply this principle to the conquering of natural phenomena in various ways. "Those who understand the Principle of Vibration have taken hold of the scepter of power."

IV. THE PRINCIPLE OF OPPOSITION

11   *"Everything is dual; everything has an opposing point; everything has its pair of opposites; like and unlike are*

> *the same; opposites are identical in nature, but different*
> *in degree; extremes bond; all truths are but partial*
> *truths; all paradoxes may be reconciled."* — Summum

12   This principle embodies the idea that everything is dual; everything has two opposing sides; everything has its pair of opposites, of which all are ancient aphorisms. It explains the paradoxes that have perplexed so many and have been stated as follows: "Thesis and antithesis are identical in nature, but different in degree"; "opposites are the same, differing only in degree"; "the pairs of opposites may be reconciled"; "in and out of bond NOTHING and POSSIBILITY meet"; "extremes bond"; "everything is and is not at the same time"; "every truth is partially false"; "all truths are a paradox"; "there are at least two sides to every story," etc. It explains that in everything, there are two opposing points or opposite aspects (complementarity), and that opposites are really only the two extremes of the same event, with many varying degrees between them. To illustrate, "hot and cold," although opposites, are really the same phenomenon, the differences consisting merely of degrees of the same "event." Look at your thermometer and see if you can discover where hot terminates and cold begins! In actuality, there is no such thing as absolute hot or absolute cold — the two terms "hot" and "cold" simply indicate varying degrees of the same event, and that same event which manifests as hot and cold is merely a form, variety, and rate of vibration. So "hot" and "cold" are simply the two opposing points of that which you call "temperature" — and the phenomena attendant thereupon are manifestations of the Principle of Opposition. The same principle is

involved in the case of "light and darkness," which are the same event, the difference consisting of varying degrees between the two opposing points of the phenomenon. Where does darkness leave off and light begin? What is the difference between "large and small," "hard and soft," "black and white," "sharp and dull," "noise and quiet," "high and low," "positive and negative?" The Principle of Opposition explains these paradoxes.

13   The same principle operates on the spiritual and mental levels. Take an example from the mental level — that of "love and hate" — two mental states apparently totally different. Yet there are degrees of hate and degrees of love, and a middle point in which you use the terms "like or dislike," which shade into each other so gradually that sometimes you are at a loss to know whether you like or dislike or neither. All are simply degrees of the same event as you will find if you will but feel it for a moment. More than this (and considered of more importance by the students), it is possible to change the vibrations of hate to the vibrations of love in one's own mind and in the minds of others. Many of you who read these lines have had personal experiences of the involuntary rapid transition from love to hate, and the reverse, in your own case and that of others. You will therefore realize the possibility of this being accomplished by the use of the Will, by means of knowing the Will. "Good and evil" are but opposing points of the same event, and the student understands the art of altering evil into good by means of an application of the Principle of Opposition.

14   In short, the Art of Immersion becomes a phase of Psychokinesis known and practiced by the ancient and

modern masters. All the Principles of Summum have an interrelationship with Opposition. Opposition draws its NATURE from the copulation of CREATION — the Big Bang if you will. An understanding of the principles will empower one to change their own vibration as well as that of others, if they will devote the time and study necessary to master the art.

V. THE PRINCIPLE OF RHYTHM

15 *"Everything flows out and in; everything has its season; all things rise and fall; the pendulum swing expresses itself in everything; the measure of the swing to the right is the measure of the swing to the left; rhythm compensates."* — Summum

16   This principle embodies the idea that in everything there exists a measured motion to and fro; an outflow and inflow; a swing backward and forward; a pendulum like movement; a tide like ebb and flow; a high tide and a low tide. All things "come in and out of bond" between the two opposing points which exist in accordance with the Principle of Opposition described previously. There is always an action and a reaction; an advance and a retreat; a rising and a sinking. This is in the affairs of the universe, suns, worlds, humankind, animals, mind, energy, and matter. This law is established in the creation and destruction of worlds; in the rise and fall of nations; and finally in the mental states of humans. The students that realize this principle find its universal application and discover the means to overcome its effect upon themselves. They apply

the mental Law of Neutralization. They cannot annul the principle or cause it to cease its operation. They do not escape the effect the principle will have on them at one level, but they have learned how to escape its effects upon themselves to a certain degree. They have learned how to USE it, instead of being USED BY it. In this and similar methods consist the art of the masters. The masters immerse themselves at the point at which they desire to rest, and then neutralize the rhythmic swing of the pendulum which wants to carry them to the opposite point. All individuals who have attained any degree of self-mastery do this naturally, more or less unconsciously, but the masters do this consciously by the use of their Will. They attain a degree of poise and mental firmness beyond belief of the masses who are swung backward and forward on the pendulum of Opposition. All the Principles of Summum have an interrelationship with Rhythm. Rhythm draws its NATURE from the copulation of CREATION. This principle and that of Opposition have been closely studied by the masters, and the method of counteracting, neutralizing, and USING them forms an important part of Psychokinesis.

VI. THE PRINCIPLE OF CAUSE & EFFECT

17 *"Every cause has its effect; every effect has its cause; everything happens according to Law; Chance is just a name for Law not recognized; there are many fields of causation, but nothing escapes the Law of Destiny."* — Summum

18   This principle embodies the idea that there is a cause for every effect; and an effect from every cause. It explains that "everything happens according to law"; that nothing ever "merely happens"; that there is no such thing as chance; that while there are various fields of cause and effect, the higher dominating the lower fields, still nothing ever entirely escapes the law (destiny). The masters understand the art and method of rising above the ordinary field of cause and effect, and by mentally rising to a higher field, they become causers instead of effects. The masses of people are carried along obedient to environment, the wills and desires of others stronger than themselves, heredity, suggestion, and other outward causes moving them about like pawns on the chessboard of life. But the masters, rising to the field above, dominate their moods, character, qualities, and powers as well as the environment surrounding them, and become movers instead of pawns. They help to PLAY THE GAME OF LIFE, instead of being played and moved about by the environment. They USE the principles instead of being used. The masters obey the causation of the higher fields, but they help to RULE on their own level.

19   All the Principles of Summum have an interrelationship with Cause and Effect. Cause "comes in and out of bond" with Effect; all EVENTS are between the cause and effect. Cause and Effect draws its NATURE from the copulation of CREATION. In this statement there is condensed a wealth of knowledge.

VII. THE PRINCIPLE OF GENDER

20 *"Gender is in everything; everything has its masculine and feminine principles; Gender manifests on all levels."*
— Summum

21   This principle embodies the idea that there is GENDER expressed in everything — the masculine and feminine principles ever at work. The NATURE of the copulation of CREATION displays in this principle. This is a fact not only of the physical level, but of the mental and even the spiritual levels. On the physical levels the principle presents itself as SEX; on the higher levels it takes higher forms, but the principle is ever the same. No creation, physical, mental, or spiritual, is possible without this principle. An understanding of its laws will throw light on many a subject that has perplexed the minds of humans.

22   The Principle of Gender works ever in the direction of generation, re-generation, and creation. Everything and every person contain the two elements or aspects of this great principle within it, him, or her. Every male thing has the female element as well; every female contains also the male principle. If you are to understand the philosophy of mental and spiritual creation, generation, and re-generation, you must understand and study this principle. All the Principles of Summum have an interrelationship with Gender. As the NOTHING "comes in" and the POSSIBILITY "out of bond," Gender is created. Gender draws its NATURE from the copulation of CREATION. It contains the solution to many mysteries of life.

An infinite number of times, point C passes between A and B in a finite moment. It has a harmony to it. You can hear it within yourself. You can hear point C passing in and out of bond between Nothingness and Totalness. It's the moment that you're alive and the moment that you are dead. But it's so fast that you believe that there's a continuum going along all the time.

— AMEN RA

CHAPTER 4

THE DIVINE PROPORTION

1   "NOTHING AND POSSIBILITY come in and out of bond infinite times in a finite moment. Yet it is impossible for two things to join in harmony or discord without the presence of a third, for a 'BOND' must exist to unite them, and this 'BOND' is 'OBJECTIVELY OBSERVED' in its relation to PROPORTION." — Summum

2   The OBJECTIVE OBSERVATION of Creation, including the principles of Psychokinesis, Correspondence, Vibration, Opposition, Rhythm, Cause and Effect, and Gender, requires a discussion of proportion; for all seven Principles of Summum can be objectively discussed in their relation to PROPORTION.

3   It is the influence of the rule of PROPORTION on the objective observer which causes humankind to ascribe to Creation human emotions, feelings, and characteristics. Through genetics, all these descriptions survive from the

days of the childhood of the race. This depiction of Creation is the natural memory held within every cell of your body inherited from the evolution of the race. You are genetically bound and bound within your essence, for it is your inheritance.

4   The objective observer, bound by the rule of PROPORTION in the examination of the existent universe, discovers both an organized universe and a universe in chaos, rational and irrational numbers, beauty and ugliness, love and hate, pleasure and pain, harmony and discord, sanity and insanity, truth and falsity. These descriptions are merely proportional effects of Opposition and the other Principles of Summum.

5   The objective observers within this universe see harmony expressed by those emotions, feelings, and characteristics present within themselves. This harmony is viewed within NATURE and the universe as THE DIVINE PROPORTION. Although the proportions seem to be fixed in NATURE, they are not. The only reason they seem fixed is because they are fixed within the observer's mind. These fixed mental vibrations dictate the observer's likes and dislikes, happiness and sadness. They also dictate one's sense of pleasure and pain, beauty and ugliness, love and hate, truth and falsity, resulting in one being captive of these memories fixed by both body and mind. For if the observer were to view NATURE from an altered state of consciousness, the proportion would also be altered. From a quantum viewpoint, multiple fields of consciousness are viewed simultaneously. If you could behold the consciousness of both a snail and a human simultaneously,

you would realize that pieces of gravel are as boulders to snails but pebbles to humans.

6   Times and lengths, space-time, and mass are all altered in proportion when the body concerned is in motion relative to the observer. In other words, moving bodies appear to be altered in terms of their shape, size, and speed, depending on your viewpoint. Apparent increase of mass in swiftly moving particles has been observed. For example, when an electron is accelerated, it appears to gain mass. Einstein's special theory of relativity embodies the mathematical essence of proportion and the interrelationship of the Principles of Summum. An altered state of consciousness makes a quantum leap beyond any fixed state of observation demonstrating that the Divine Proportion is also subject to the law of Paradox and only partial truth.

7   The Divine Proportion ascribed to the collective consciousness of your state of evolution has been expressed, "For of three (3) magnitudes, if the greatest (AB) is to the mean (CB) as the mean (CB) is to the least (AC), they therefore all shall be one."

NOTHING   **POSSIBILITY**

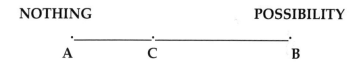

A   C   B

8   Modern science calculates the joining and splitting apart of "string proportions" (EVENTS) as the source of Creation. The elementary particles observed by science represent excitation modes of strings. This leaves us with the question, "What creates the strings?" It is the subjective copulation of Nothing and Possibility that produces these

vibrating string proportions in all their modes of excitation. As mentioned before, Creation cannot be examined in its source objectively for it requires a philosophical examination. Any examination in a material form is limited by time based dimensional space and creation's manifestation is infinitely dimensional. At this point, it is left up to the student to fill in the details of their understanding of the mathematics of the Divine Proportion, also known as the Golden Section, Phi, the Magic Ratio, the Additive Series, etc. There is available plentiful published material which, when investigated by the student, will initiate them to an understanding of the Divine Proportion.

9   The Divine Proportion can be found throughout this universe; from the swirls of galaxies to the swirls of quarks; from the harmony of music to the very physical nature of Creation. The Divine Proportion is seen as the beauty and organization in nature, the harmony and glue holding the unity of the universe. This beauty is the quality or combination of qualities which affords keen pleasure to the senses, especially that of sight or that which charms the intellectual faculties.

10   The states of discord, insanity, and chaos in the universe are observations of states seemingly opposed to the accepted Divine Proportion. Yet this is a singularly human point of view. For within chaos is found organization, within the irrational is found the rational, within ugliness is found beauty, within hate is found love, within pain is found pleasure, within discord is found harmony, within insanity is found sanity, within falsity is found truth. In reality, all discord and chaos are human judgments of their perception of a state of consciousness in opposition to the

Divine Proportion. Death and dissolution may appear as states of discord, and from the point of the fixed mind seem out of harmony.

11 The masters are not bound by these judgments which restrict the normal human being. For they have set themselves free from the lower law of a single viewpoint and observe existence from a quantum viewpoint within the same moment. The masters freely observe SUMMUM unencumbered by the constraints of the fixed mind.

12 The construct of "proper" time in each personal self-perspective (the individual) and in the collective viewpoint (humankind) accounts for the universal acceptance of this Divine Proportion. This construct is seen as a narrow, single viewing point from which only a small portion of the total can be observed. It is the frame of reference from which observations are made and by which the Divine Proportion is identified. But as the frame of reference (consciousness) expands, so does the Divine Proportion or observation thereof expand. For as all manifest things evolve, so do the proportions of the Divine Proportion evolve. As the mental vibrations of those examining Creation change, so does the Divine Proportion change.

13 An understanding of the relationship of PROPORTION to the seven Principles of Summum will enable the student to master the principles.

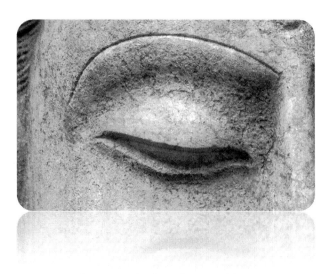

There can't be chaos without order and order without chaos. They need each other to exist. So what you do is you find yourself and find where you're at. Then find the neutral position, and from there, you can put things in any condition you want. But if you judge it as being bad, automatically, you're in the bad with it. If you judge it as being neutral, that's the safe position to look at things. Then you take it from there, and you transform it into a good thing.

— AMEN RA

CHAPTER 5

PSYCHOKINESIS

1   "Mind (as well as metal and elements) may be altered psychokinetically, from state to state; degree to degree; proportion to proportion; condition to condition; point to point; vibration to vibration. Psychokinesis is Mental Mastery." — Summum

2   Alchemists, astrologers, parapsychologists, and psychologists have always existed. From the art of ancient astrology has grown modern astronomy; from alchemy, modern chemistry; and esoteric psychology has evolved into the modern institutes of psychology. Do not assume that the ancients were ignorant of that which modern institutions presume to be their exclusive and special property. The hieroglyphs of ancient Egypt show irrefutably that the ancients had a thorough knowledge of these sciences. The very design of the pyramids is a study in astronomical science. The ancients also had an understanding of chemistry, for the remnants of the ancient writings

show a familiarity with the chemical properties of elements. Modern science is verifying the ancient theories regarding physics through mathematics and experimentation. Ancient references indicate a vibratory nature behind all phenomena. Today, modern science regards the theory of matter [and energy] being formed from vibrations as fact. In addition, do not assume that the ancients were naive of the supposed modern discoveries in psychology. The ancients were skilled in the science of psychology, especially that of parapsychology, an area most modern institutes ignore.

3   The fact is that in addition to the understanding of physical science, the ancients enjoyed a knowledge of transcendental astronomy, called astrology; of transcendental chemistry, called alchemy; of transcendental psychology, called parapsychology. They enjoyed the esoteric knowledge as well as the exoteric knowledge, while modern science only subscribes to the exoteric. Among the many branches of knowledge possessed by the ancients, that known as Psychokinesis is the subject matter of this chapter.

4   "Transmutation" and "alchemy" are terms normally employed to designate the ancient art of the alteration of metals, particularly that of changing the base metals into gold. "Transubstantiation" refers to the changing of one substance into another. The word, "Psychokinesis," means the ability to influence, alter events, or change one form, species, condition, nature, or substance into another via mental processes. Therefore, Psychokinesis is the art of changing mental states, forms, and conditions into others. Psychokinesis is the Art of Mental Chemistry or parapsy-

chology, especially in its aspect of study termed "mind over matter." This is of greater significance than you may imagine. Psychokinesis, alchemy, or chemistry are important enough in their physical effects upon the mental field, but it must be realized that their effects are also felt at the spiritual level.

5   The first of the seven Summum principles is the Principle of Psychokinesis, the axiom of which is, "SUMMUM is MIND; the universe is a mental creation." It means that the underlying essence of the universe is mind, and the universe itself is mental, that is, "existing in the Mind of SUMMUM." This principle shall be considered in succeeding chapters, but for now the effect of the principle can be examined if you assume it to be fact.

6   If CREATION is mental in its nature, then Psychokinesis must be the art of CHANGING THE CONDITIONS OF THE UNIVERSES in their fields of space-time, matter, force, and mind, affecting the quantum potential. This Psychokinesis is really the "magic" of which the ancient writers had so much to say in their mystical works and about which they gave so few practical instructions. If all is mental, then the art which empowers one to alter mental conditions must also render the master the "controller of material conditions" as well as those ordinarily called "mental."

7   Only the advanced masters of Psychokinesis have been able to attain the degree of power necessary to control the grosser physical conditions such as the control of the weather, the production or cessation of tempests, earthquakes, and other physical phenomena. These perfections known as supranatural powers are attained through spiritual evolution. Masters of these perfections attain a level

of spirituality which allows them to sever the normal bonds with which the forces of nature bind humankind. In control of the forces of nature, the masters are empowered to know the minds of others, break the bonds of light and thus to disappear, overcome the force of gravity and levitate, see into the heart of atoms, etc. Such human types have existed and do exist today. Students have witnessed the author of this work psychokinetically altering nature, and have written testimonials to the fact of this phenomenon. The masters DO NOT make public exhibitions of their powers, but seek seclusion from the crowds in order to better work their way along the path of evolution. For the masters have evolved to these powers through many incarnations wherein they worked to develop this potential within their Will. These powers are entirely mental, and operate along the fields of higher mental function under the Summum Principle of Psychokinesis, "The universe is mental." — Summum.

8   The students of lesser degree than masters — the initiates and teachers — are able to freely work along the mental fields with Psychokinesis. In fact, all that is named "psychic phenomena," "mental influence," "mental science," "new age phenomena," etc., operates along the same general fields, for there is but one principle involved regardless of what name the phenomenon is called.

9   The students and practitioners of Psychokinesis work among mental fields, altering mental conditions and states according to various mental practices. The popular and diverse "subliminals," "affirmations," and "refutations" utilized by the current and predominant discipline of mental science are but formulas, quite imperfect and unscientific.

The majority of modern practitioners are uneducated compared to the very few masters, for they lack the components of the knowledge upon which the work is based. They refuse to put forth the effort and work necessary to attain the knowledge in its entirety. These individuals lack an appetite for the knowledge and thus do not hunger or thirst for it. Unable to hold their attention on the knowledge, they remain preoccupied with the self-interests of their personalities.

10   Not only may the mental states of one's self be changed by Psychokinesis, the states of others may be and are constantly altered in the same way. Among the masses, these changes occur, for the most part, unconsciously. But when one understands the laws and principles, the change is often a conscious one. The mental states of people who are not informed of the principles are extremely easy to affect. Many students and practitioners of modern mental science know that every material condition which depends upon the state of mind of other people may be altered. These alterations are in accordance with the earnest desire and will of the master and the masses. For one is doing the altering and the other desires the alteration. The purpose at this point is merely to show the principle and art underlying all of these various forms of practice, good and evil, for the force may be used in opposite directions according to the Principle of Opposition.

11   The Principle of Psychokinesis has been stated so that all who read may possess the Master Key that will unlock the many doors to the Principle of Opposition.

Question: *Rather than treating this as a form of belief, how does one experience its reality?*

Answer: Through meditations that allow one to resonate on the center, point C, vibration – the harmonic resonation of Phi. You experience it. It talks back to you and it shows itself to you totally within nature. This comes through submission to it. You experience it through work, through meditation.

— AMEN RA

CHAPTER 6

SUMMUM

1   "Under and behind the universe of space-time and change is the Substantial Essence — Creation's Copulation." — Summum

2   "Substantial" means, "real; actual; true; not imaginary." "Essence" means, "that which makes something what it is; intrinsic, fundamental nature or most important quality."

3   Within the esoteric, under and behind all outward appearances or expressions, there must always be a substantial essence. This is the law. Considering the universe of which you are a unit, you see nothing but change in matter, forces, and mental states. You see that nothing really IS, but that everything is BECOMING and CHANGING. Nothing stands still. Everything is born, grows, and dies. The very instant anything reaches its height, it begins to decline. The law of Rhythm is in constant operation. There is no consistent reality, no enduring quality, no fixity, no

substantiality in anything. Nothing is permanent but change. You observe all things evolving from other things and resolving into other things — a constant action and reaction; inflow and outflow; building up and tearing down; creation and destruction; birth and death. Nothing endures but change. If you are a thinking person, you realize that all of these changing things must be but outward appearances or expressions of some underlying power — some substantial essence.

4   All thinkers in all lands for all times have assumed the necessity for postulating the existence of this substantial essence. All philosophies worthy of the name have been based upon this thought. People have given to this substantial essence many names. Some have called it by the term of deity (under many titles). Others have called it "The Infinite Eternal Energy." Others have called it "Love." But all have acknowledged its existence. It is self-evident — it needs no argument. It is looked for in the questions, "Where did I come from?" "Why am I here?" "How did God come into being?" "Where did the universe come from?"

5   This book follows the examples of the Masters by identifying this underlying power — this substantial essence which emanates from the bonding of Nothing and Possibility — with the names "SUMMUM" and "Creation's Copulation." In this chapter it will be called SUMMUM, which will be considered the most comprehensive term for this discussion.

6   It is taught by the great thinkers of all times, as well as by the Summa Individuals, that the esoteric nature of SUMMUM is UNKNOWABLE by humankind. This must

be so, for otherwise SUMMUM Itself would not understand Its own nature if It were humankind. For humankind is not SUMMUM and to completely understand a thing one must be that thing, not just an observer of the thing. This is not to say, however, that the esoteric nature of SUMMUM cannot ever be known. There are states of being in which it is known, and humankind, in time, will progress to these states, but will have long since passed the point of humanity.

7   SUMMUM, "in Itself," is and must ever be UNKNOWABLE to humankind. Only the EXOTERIC NATURE of SUMMUM can be known. As explained in chapter two, SUMMUM is "NOTHING AND POSSIBILITY come in and out of bond infinite times in a finite moment." "It takes the joining of TWO to make one — SUMMUM." This is the "Copulation of Creation." Only the whole of SUMMUM can understand Itself totally. However, the human being can understand SUMMUM based upon its experience as a unit of SUMMUM.

8   There are those who ascribe to SUMMUM the personality, qualities, properties, characteristics, and attributes of themselves. These ascriptions are not worthy of grown men and women, and represent ideas that are simply illusions about the substantial essence of SUMMUM. However, it is understandable because humans can only make pronouncements about Creation from their limited point of view. These ideas are simply illusions about the substantial essence of SUMMUM.

9   While the totality of SUMMUM is unknowable to humankind, there are certain facts connected with Its existence which the human mind finds itself compelled to

accept. An examination of these facts forms a proper subject of inquiry, particularly as they agree with the explanation given by the Summa Individuals.

10 The human reason informs you as follows regarding SUMMUM:

11 **(1)** SUMMUM must be ALL that REALLY IS. NOTHING exists outside of SUMMUM and NOTHING exists inside of SUMMUM, for SUMMUM is and is not; the law of Paradox.

12 **(2)** SUMMUM is INFINITE and FINITE, for there is nothing to define, confine, bound, limit, or restrict SUMMUM. It is automatically created and has always continuously existed and not existed, for there is nothing else to have ever created It. Its expressed states are infinite in space. It is everywhere, for there is no place outside of SUMMUM. It cannot be otherwise than continuous in space, for It creates all space. It is without break, cessation, separation, or interruption, for there is nothing to break, separate, or interrupt Its continuity, and nothing with which to "fill in the gaps." It must be infinite in power and absolute, for there is nothing to limit, restrict, confine, disturb, or condition It. It is subject to no other power, for there is no other power. Although, SUMMUM is also NOTHING as It alternates from (SUMMUM) POSSIBILITY to NOTHING — the Principle of Rhythm.

13 **(3)** SUMMUM is IMMUTABLE and not subject to change in Its essence nature, for there is nothing to work

changes upon It; nothing into which It could change or from which It could have changed. It cannot be added to or subtracted from; increased or diminished; or become greater or lesser in any respect whatsoever. It must have always been and must always remain just what It is now, SUMMUM. There has never been, is not now, and never will be anything else into which It can change.

14   SUMMUM being infinite and finite, absolute, eternal, and unchangeable, it must follow that anything changeable, fleeting, and conditioned cannot be SUMMUM. As there is nothing outside or inside of SUMMUM, then any and all such finite things must be as nothing in reality. Now do not become confused, for there is a reconciliation of this apparently contradictory philosophy. Be patient. You will reach it in time.

15   You see around you that which you call matter, which forms the physical foundation for all forms. Is SUMMUM merely matter? No! Matter cannot display life or mind, for nothing rises higher than its own source. Nothing is ever reflected in an effect that is not in the cause. Nothing is evolved as a consequent that is not involved as an antecedent. Modern science informs you that there is really no such thing as matter — that which is called matter is merely "energy equaling mass multiplied by the square of the velocity of light." In other words, energy or force at a "proper" time, as a low rate of vibration, results in matter. All science has accepted the idea that matter is a state of energy, and energy is the EVENT between a cause and effect.

16   Is SUMMUM mere energy or force? Again, no. For life can never evolve from blind energy or force. Nothing can rise higher than its source. Nothing is evolved unless it is involved. Nothing displays in the effect unless it is in the cause. So SUMMUM cannot be mere energy or force, for if It were, there would be no life, intelligence, or mind in existence, and common sense would tell you better than that. You are alive and using mind to consider this very question and so are those who claim that energy or force is everything.

17   What is there then, behind or higher than matter or energy that you know to be existent in the universe? LIFE and MIND and INTELLIGENCE! Life and mind in all their varying degrees of unfoldment!

18   Just as life and mind are that much higher than the mechanical forces which govern matter, this LIVING MIND is so far above and beyond anything which mortals can know — INFINITE, LIVING MIND as compared to finite life and mind. It is the concept of INFINITE, LIVING MIND which the Summa Individuals refer to when they use the word "SPIRIT!"

19   SUMMUM is INFINITE, LIVING MIND — the Summa Individuals call It SPIRIT!

Nothingness is the womb and total possibility is a little larger than the womb. It's because there is more possibility than nothingness. That's why there's more matter than antimatter, and why we're all here. If there was more nothingness, there wouldn't be anything and you wouldn't be here. This is the Phi equation. The larger side is the projection of possibility and nothingness is the womb. The projection of possibility enters the womb and copulates an infinite number of times in a finite moment causing a resonation. The resonation comes out, which is the Word.

— AMEN RA

CHAPTER 7

THE MENTAL UNIVERSE

1   **"The universe is mental, emanating from the Mind of SUMMUM." — Summum**

2   SUMMUM is SPIRIT! What is spirit? This question needs to be examined at this point. Spirit is the effect of the EVENT in which the two grand opposites are poised in opposition or SUBJECTIVE OBSERVATION to one another. This EVENT is such that the cause (the bonding of NOTHING and POSSIBILITY) and the resulting effect (spirit) occur simultaneously (SUMMUM). Spirit is the "life" force energy produced as a result of Creation's observation of Itself (the copulation).

3   The process of observation or attention, direct or indirect, establishes the foundation of the structure of Creation. The collective consciousness of the units of Creation establishes the presence of the universe. It is similar to the human body, in which billions of individual cells (units) make it up to be what it is. As the cells within the body

change, so does the condition of the body change. The mental condition of all material existence alters with the mental condition (consciousness) of all the units of the existent material universe.

4   Spirit is a name that humankind gives to the concept of infinite, living mind; the essence of Creation; the BOND between NOTHING and POSSIBILITY; the joining together and splitting apart of the mental "string proportions" of the subjective NOTHING and POSSIBILITY. It can be called the "real essence." It means living mind. It is as much superior to life and mind as you know them, as the latter are superior to mechanical energy and matter. Spirit transcends your understanding, and you use the term merely that you may think or speak of SUMMUM. For the purpose of thought and understanding at this point, you are justified in thinking of spirit as infinite, living mind; at the same time acknowledging that you are examining it from the consciousness of a human being. It is best to admit this limitation, for when you acknowledge your position, you are free to travel the road of discovery.

5   Now proceed to a consideration of the nature of the universe as a whole and its parts. What is the universe? You have seen that there can be nothing outside of SUMMUM. Then is the universe SUMMUM? No, it is not. The universe seems to be made up of MANY UNITS and is constantly changing. In this sense it does not measure up or conform to ideas as previously stated. For if the universe is not SUMMUM, it must be nothing. Such is the logical conclusion of the mind at first thought based upon the argument presented to this point. This will not satisfy the question, for you are aware of the existence of the uni-

verse. Then if the universe is not SUMMUM, must it be nothing?

6   If the universe exists at all or seems to exist, it must proceed in some way from SUMMUM. It must be an emanation from SUMMUM, for something cannot come from nothing alone. From what could SUMMUM have created it? Some philosophers have answered this question by saying that SUMMUM created the universe from ITSELF, that is, from the being and essence of SUMMUM. This will not do, for SUMMUM cannot be subtracted from or divided, altered or modified. Then again if this be so, would not each particle in the universe be aware of its being SUMMUM? SUMMUM could not lose Its knowledge of Itself, or actually become an atom, or blind force, or lowly living thing. Some humans, realizing that SUMMUM is EVERYTHING and recognizing that they exist, have jumped to the conclusion that they and SUMMUM are identical. They have filled the air with shouts of "I AM GOD!" to the laughter of the public and the sorrow of the sages. The claim of the cell that "I am the human!" would be modest in comparison.

7   What is the universe if it is not SUMMUM, not created by SUMMUM having separated Itself into fragments? What else could it be? Of what else can it be made? This is a great question. Examine it carefully. You find here that the Principle of Correspondence will come to your assistance. The old axiom, "As above, so below," may be employed at this point. Venture to get a glimpse of the workings on higher fields by examining those on your own. The Principle of Correspondence must apply to this as well as to other obstacles.

8   On their own field of being, how do humans create? Firstly, they may create by making something from external materials. This will not suffice, for there are no materials outside of SUMMUM with which It may create. Secondly, humans pro-create or reproduce their kind by sexual reproduction or cloning, which are self-multiplications accomplished by transferring a portion of their substance to their offspring. This will not do, because SUMMUM cannot transfer or subtract a portion of Itself. Nor can It reproduce or multiply Itself. In the first place there would be a taking away, and in the second case a multiplication or addition to SUMMUM, both sets of circumstances being an impossibility. However, there is a third way in which humans create. They CREATE MENTALLY! In so doing, they use no outside materials nor do they reproduce themselves. Yet their spirit pervades their mental creation.

9   Allowing for the Principle of Correspondence, you are justified in considering that SUMMUM creates the universe MENTALLY, in a manner akin to the process whereby humans create mental images. This is the only logical answer which is also the one given by the Summa Individuals. Such are the teachings of Summum. SUMMUM can create in no other way except mentally, without either using material (for there is none to use outside of Itself) or else reproducing Itself (which is also impossible). There is no escape from this conclusion of the reason which agrees with the highest teaching of the Summa Individuals. Just as you may create a universe of your own in your mentality, so does SUMMUM create universes in Its own mentality. Although your creation is the mental creation of a finite mind, that of SUMMUM is the creation of an Infinite Mind.

The two are similar in kind, but infinitely different in degree. You shall examine more closely this process of creation and manifestation as you proceed. At this point fix in your mind, THE UNIVERSE AND ALL IT CONTAINS IS A MENTAL CREATION OF SUMMUM. Truly, EVERYTHING IS MIND!

10   A point needs to be made regarding the concept of "mind." Humankind tends to correlate the idea of mind with "thinking." This occurs because most humankind are constantly engaged in thoughts concerning their physical body life. Because their attention is wrapped up and fixated in thought, they cannot observe anything more to their minds other than their own thinking; and they have great difficulty considering concepts of mind outside of having thoughts and the thinking process.

11   There is far more to the human mind than humans realize. The concept of mind within the Summum philosophy has a broader meaning that goes beyond the idea of thinking. While it is accurate to say the human mind is similar in nature to the Mind of Creation (via the Principle of Correspondence), the Mind of Creation is infinitely different in degree.

12   The Mind of Creation is not a "thinking" mind but has all thought contained within it in silence. Thought is an event and all events are produced by the copulating bond between the Grand Opposites, NOTHING and POSSIBILITY. Infinite events within the finite moment — this describes the Mind of Creation (SUMMUM). When SUMMUM expresses into manifest form the infinite events, time and action appear. Within the action is where "thinking" occurs, among the individualized units that are created. The ex-

pression is within SUMMUM but the expression is not SUMMUM. The expression is part of the Mind's essence projected out into its mental womb.

13   Consider this paradox. Surrounded by nothing is all possibility (SUMMUM), and the Mind of Creation rests in the nothingness with everything in it. Thought and action while held inside are outside the Mind of Creation.

14   **"SUMMUM creates in Its Infinite Mind infinite universes which exist for aeons of SPACE-TIME; and yet to SUMMUM, the creation, development, decline, and death of a billion universes is as the time of the twinkling of an eye." — Summum**

15   The finite moment in which NOTHING and POSSIBIL-ITY come in and out of bond an infinite number of times has always existed. It always was, is now, and always will be. The moment holds the Mind of Creation. The moment is the Mind of Creation. Within the Mind, Creation projects a portion of its essence into its mental womb and expresses or manifests the essence into space-time, form, and action. Infinite universes are created and each one goes through its sequence of birth, growth, deterioration, and death. Then the Mind withdraws the projection back into itself. The process repeats for it is a neverending cycle just as the copulation between NOTHING and POSSIBILITY is neverending.

16   The Principle of Gender is manifested in all fields of life; material, mental, and spiritual. As you have seen before, "gender" does not just mean "sex." Sex is a material expression of gender. "Gender" means "relating to generation or

creation." In any field, the Principle of Gender must be manifested. This is true even in the creation of universes.

17   For example, there are male and female "Gods" or creators that act in some of the infinite dimensional fields created by SUMMUM. The Summum philosophy is that SUMMUM, in Itself, is above Gender, as It is THE LAW from which the laws proceed and It is not subject to them. Although the essence of the law is found within SUMMUM, the copulation of Nothing and Possibility can be looked upon as the essence of Gender. When SUMMUM causes manifestation, then It ACTS according to law and principle, for It moves on a lower level and field of being. Consequently, It exhibits the Principle of Gender in Its essence — in Its masculine and feminine aspects — primarily at the mental level and secondarily, on the physical level.

18   In your mundane concepts you have spoken of the Fatherhood of God and the Motherhood of Nature — of God, the Divine Father, and Nature the Universal Mother — and thus have instinctively acknowledged the Principle of Gender in the universe.

19   SUMMUM is not real duality; only in Its subjective essence. The two aspects come from NOTHING and POSSIBILITY in their BONDing copulation; for SUMMUM is the EVENT of this bond. The masculine principle displayed by SUMMUM stands, in a way, apart from the actual mental creation of the universe. It projects Its Will toward the feminine principle, the womb (which may be called "nature"), whereupon the latter begins the actual work of the creation of the universe. From the BIG BANG come the simple states of vibratory energies; extending to humans and on and on still higher; all according to well

established and firmly enforced laws of nature. If you prefer the old figure of thought, you may think of the masculine principle as "God, the Father," and of the feminine principle as "Mother Nature," from whose womb all created things have been born. This is more than a mere poetic figure of speech. It is an idea of the actual process of the generation of the universe. Always remember that SUMMUM is but One. Only in Its subjective essence is It dual, and in Its Infinite Mind the universe is generated and exists.

20 It will help to get the proper idea if you will apply the law of Correspondence to yourself and your own mind. You know that the part of you which you call "I" stands, in a sense, apart, and observes the generation of mental images in your own mind. The part of your mind in which the mental generation is accomplished may be called the "Me." It is in distinction from the "I" which stands and witnesses and examines the thoughts, ideas, and images of the "Me." Remember, "As above, so below," and the phenomena of one level may be employed to solve the riddles of higher or lower levels.

21 Is it any wonder that you, the child, feel that instinctive reverence for SUMMUM; the feeling you call "religion"; the respect and reverence for THE FATHER MIND? Is it any wonder, when you consider the works and wonders of nature, that you are overcome with a mighty feeling which has its roots deep in your esoteric being? It is THE MOTHER MIND that you are pressing close up to like a babe to the breast.

22 Do not make the mistake of supposing that the world you see around you, Earth, which is a mere grain of dust in

the universe, is the universe itself. There are billions upon billions of such worlds and greater. There are billions and billions of such universes in existence within the Infinite Mind of SUMMUM. Even in your small solar system there are dimensions and fields of life so much higher than yours that, by comparison, earthbound mortals are as but the basic life forms that dwell on the ocean's bed. There are beings with powers and attributes higher than humankind has ever dreamed of the gods possessing. Yet these beings were once as you and still lower; and in time, you will be even as they and still higher. For such is the DESTINY of humankind as stated by the Summa Individuals.

23 Death is not real, not even in the relative sense. It is but birth to a new life. When you leave your body, you progress to another field of life. You go on, and on, and on, to higher and still higher levels of life, for aeons of time. As you make this epic journey, you reach a point where you are able to choose and create each new life. By using higher law against lower laws, your creation of a new life becomes divine. This guided transference of your spirit from this life to the next is the glory of your intelligence. The glory of the transference is the glory of a god.

24 Just as it is impossible to destroy matter (only transform its nature), it is impossible for death to destroy you. The universe is your home and you shall explore its furthest recesses before the end of time. You are dwelling in the Infinite Mind of SUMMUM, and your possibilities and opportunities are infinite both in time and space. At the end of the Grand Cycle of Aeons, when SUMMUM shall draw back into Itself all of Its generation, you will go gladly, for you will then know the whole truth of being at one with

SUMMUM. Such is the statement of the Summa Individuals, those who have advanced well along the Path.

25   In the meantime, rest calm and serene. You are held by the infinite power of the FATHER-MOTHER MIND (Destiny).

There's always a paradox going on in life. No matter what aspect of life you're in, there's a paradox in it. It doesn't make any difference unless you transcend the paradox. From the beginning, all teachers who understood the paradox have spoken. They said that you need to take the exterior and turn it into the interior, and take the interior and turn it into the exterior, and make them into a oneness.

— AMEN RA

CHAPTER 8

THE DIVINE PARADOX

1   "The universe IS NOT, still IT IS; everything is
dual; everything has at least two sides; all truths
are but partial truths." — Summum

2   This is the Divine Paradox of the universe. It is an effect
of the Principle of Opposition and is established when
the process of SUMMUM generates. SUMMUM receives
Its nature from the "NOTHING AND POSSIBILITY come
in and out of bond infinite times in a finite moment." The
Divine Paradox has to do with duality, for when you talk
about anything in Creation, you must talk about the TWO
creating one. The bonding of POSSIBILITY and NOTHING
results in the displayed Creation; to take a microcosmic
example, it takes the bonding of the male with the female
to create new life.

3   The partially wise, recognizing the comparative unreality of the universe, imagine that they may escape its laws.
Such is vanity, for these presumptuous fools are broken

and torn apart by the elements by reason of their folly. The truly wise, knowing the nature of the universe, use Law against laws; the higher against the lower; and by the Art of Psychokinesis alter that which is undesirable into that which is perfected, and thus prevail. Mastery consists not in abnormal dreams, visions, and fantastic imaginings or living, but in using the higher forces against the lower; escaping the pains of the lower field by rising to the higher; always remembering DESTINY and realizing the fields are fixed in cause and effect. Psychokinesis, not presumptuous denial, is the tool of the master.

4   To THE INFINITE SUMMUM, this universe, its laws, its powers, its life, its phenomena are as things witnessed in a state of meditation. Yet to all that is finite, the universe must be treated as real. Life, action, and thought must be based thereupon, accordingly, although with an ever increasing understanding of the higher states; each according to its own level and laws. It has been postulated that SUMMUM dreams or imagines. This is impossible, for the essence of SUMMUM is fixed in ITSELF and cannot be added to or taken from. When human beings live, act, and think of the universe as merely a dream (like their own finite dreams), then certainly it becomes so for them. Like sleep walkers they stumble ever around and around in circles, making no progress, and are forced into an awakening at last by their falling bruised and bleeding over the natural laws which they have ignored. Keep your mind ever alert on the stars, but let your eyes watch over your footsteps. Otherwise you will fall into the mud by reason of your upward gaze. Remember the Divine Paradox, that while the universe IS NOT, still IT IS. Remember ever the

two opposing points of Truth — the essence of the Absolute and the Relative. Be aware of partial truths.

5   The Law of Paradox is an aspect of the Principle of Opposition. Opposition draws its nature from the essence of SUMMUM, and SUMMUM is generated by the copulation of Creation. Therefore, the Law of Paradox exhibits the realm of the opposites — NOTHING and POSSIBILITY in their copulating bond. In classical physics, waves and particles were all that existed, and everything was either one or the other. The ability of quantum particles to assume the character of either, depending upon the experiment conducted, constitutes a seemingly inexplicable paradox of the quantum world. Observations of light acting as both a particle and a wave is a classic example and illustrates the complementarity that exists within all created things.

6   The ancient writings are filled with references to the appearance of the paradox in the consideration of the problem of life and being. The teachers are constantly warning their students against the error of omitting the "other side" of the story or question. Their warnings are particularly directed to the problem of the essence of the Absolute and the Relative which perplex all students of philosophy, and which cause so many to think and act contrary to what is generally known as "common sense."

7   The first thought that comes to thinking humans after they realize that the universe is a mental creation of SUMMUM, is that the universe and all that it contains is a mere illusion; an unreality; against which their instincts naturally revolt. This problem, like all others, must be considered both from the essence of the Absolute and Relative

points of view. From the viewpoint of the Absolute, the universe is in the nature of an illusion, an aspect, a phantasmagoria as compared to SUMMUM in Itself. Just as you may have very intense dream states, you seldom mistake your dreams for the reality of who you are upon waking. You even recognize this when you speak of the world of action as a "play" — you are one of the actors playing — you are born, you come and go, strut and fret, and then you die. The element of impermanence and change, finiteness and unsubstantiality, must ever be connected with the idea of a created universe when it is contrasted with the idea of SUMMUM — no matter what your beliefs may be concerning the nature of both. The thought is found in all forms of philosophical and religious conceptions, as well as in the theories of the respective schools of metaphysics and theology.

8 Summum's teachings do not proclaim the unsubstantiality of the universe in any stronger terms than those more familiar to you, although the presentation of the subject may seem somewhat more startling. Anything that has a beginning and an ending must be, by definition, impermanent. The universe comes under the rule in all disciplines of thought. From the essence of the Absolute point of view, there is nothing real except SUMMUM, no matter what you may use in thinking of or discussing the subject. Whether the universe be created of matter, or whether it be a mental creation in the Mind of SUMMUM, it is unsubstantial, nonenduring, a thing of space-time and change. You want to realize this fact thoroughly before you pass judgment on the Summum conception of the mental na-

ture of the universe. Think over any and all of the other conceptions and see whether this be not a fact of them.

9   The essence of the Absolute point of view shows merely one side of the picture. The other side is the Relative one. The essence of Absolute Fact has been defined as "things as the mind of God knows them," while Relative Fact as "things as the highest human being understands them." While to SUMMUM, the universe must be unreal and illusionary, a mere aspect or result of expression. Nevertheless, to the finite minds forming a part of that universe and viewing it through mortal faculties, the universe is very real and must be so considered. The report of the Summa Individuals is that your difficulty with the Principle of Paradox is that the finite human mind observes one thing at a moment, while the Infinite Mind of SUMMUM observes all moments as one. There are infinite degrees of observation between the human and SUMMUM. In recognizing the essence of Absolute View, you must not make the mistake of ignoring or denying the facts and phenomena of the universe as they present themselves to your mortal faculties. Remember, you are not SUMMUM.

10   Take a familiar illustration. You all recognize the fact that matter exists to your senses. You will not manage very well if you do not. Yet even your finite minds understand the scientific dictum that there is strictly no such thing as matter from a scientific point of view. What is called matter is held to be merely a composite of atoms made of subatomic particles, which themselves are simply a grouping of units of force and energy vibrating and in constant orbital motion. Your scientists build a superconducting supercollider to find ever smaller particles of matter as

they look for clues to the creation of the universe. However, it would be just as well to explore space, as inner and outer space are both ruled by the same laws. In reality there is no such thing as smallest or largest — size is infinite in both respects. "Large and small" are just aspects of the same event.

11 You kick a stone and you feel the impact. It seems to be real and you know it to be what has been stated above. But remember that your foot, which feels the impact by means of your brain, is likewise matter, and for that matter so is your brain. At best, one could say if it were not for the calculations of your brain, you would not know the foot or stone at all.

12 The visualizations of the artist or sculptor, as they endeavor to reproduce in stone or on canvas, seem very real to them. So do the characters in the mind of the author or dramatist, which they seek to express so that others may recognize them. If this is true in the case of your finite minds, what is the degree of reality in the mental images created in the Mind of the Infinite? To mortals, this universe of mentality is very real. It is the one you know, though you rise from level to level, higher and higher in the understanding of it. To know it otherwise than by actual experience, you must be SUMMUM Itself. It is true that the higher you rise in the scale, the nearer to "the Mind of the Father" you reach — the more apparent becomes the illusory nature of finite things. Not until SUMMUM finally draws you into Itself does the vision actually vanish.

13 You need not dwell upon the feature of illusion. Rather, recognize the real nature of the universe. Seek to under-

stand its mental laws. Endeavor to use them to the best effect in your upward progress through life as you travel from level to level of being. The laws of the universe are nonetheless "fixed laws" because of the mental nature. Everything except SUMMUM is bound by them, and the essence of SUMMUM is the Laws. What is IN THE INFINITE MIND OF SUMMUM is REAL in a degree second only to that reality itself which is held in the essence of SUMMUM.

14   You are all HELD FIRMLY IN THE INFINITE MIND OF SUMMUM and there is nothing to harm you or for you to fear. There is no power outside of SUMMUM to affect you, so you may rest calm and secure. There is a world of comfort, security, and peace in this realization when attained. Then you will sleep calmly and peacefully, rocked in the Cradle of the Deep — resting safely on the bosom of the Ocean of Infinite Mind which is SUMMUM. Truly, in SUMMUM do you live, move, and have your being.

15   Matter is still matter to you while you dwell in the field of matter. Although, you know it to be merely as composite energy or strings of force vibrating rapidly and whirling around each other, forming quanta particles within atoms. The atoms in turn vibrate and whirl forming molecules which in turn form larger masses of matter. Matter does not become less matter when you follow the inquiry still further and learn from these teachings that the force, of which the energy is but units, is merely an EVENT between a cause and effect relationship. Further, this EVENT is just a manifestation of the Mind of SUMMUM, and like all else in the universe is purely mental in its nature.

16   While in the field of matter, you must recognize its phenomena. You may control matter (as all masters of higher or lesser degree do), but you do so by applying the higher forces. You commit a folly when you attempt to deny the existence of matter in the relative aspect. You may deny its mastery over you and rightly so. But you should not attempt to ignore it in its relative aspect — at least so long as you reside within its field. For example, you do not stand in the street and allow vehicles to run you down just because you understand that they are composed of "metal," which is merely an alloy of different elements vibrating at known frequencies.

17   Nor do the laws of nature become less constant or effective when you know them to be merely mental creations. They are in full effect in the various fields. You overcome the lower laws by applying still higher ones — and in this way only. You CANNOT ESCAPE Law or rise above it entirely. Nothing but SUMMUM can escape Law — and that is because SUMMUM is LAW Itself from which all laws emerge. The most advanced masters acquire the abilities usually attributed to the gods of humankind. There are countless degrees of being in the great hierarchy of life whose power transcends even that of the highest masters among humankind, and to a magnitude unthinkable by mortals. Yet even the highest masters and the highest beings must yield to the Law and be as NOTHING in the eye of SUMMUM. If even these highest beings whose powers greatly exceed those attributed by humankind to their gods — if even these are bound by and are subservient to Law, then imagine the presumption of mortal humans of your race and degree who dare to consider

the laws of nature as unreal. Because they happen to be able to grasp the fact that the laws are mental in nature and are simply mental creations of SUMMUM, they feel they can be disregarded. Those laws which SUMMUM emanates as governing laws are not to be defied or argued away. So long as the universe endures will they endure. For the universe exists by virtue of these laws which form its framework and hold it together.

18   The Summum Principle of Psychokinesis, while explaining the nature of the universe upon the principle that all is mental, does not change the scientific conceptions of the universe, life, or evolution. Science often corroborates these Summum teachings, except for the theory of the mental creation of the universe. Summum teaches that the nature of the universe is mental, while modern science teaches that it is material, or, more recently, energy. So the student of Summum need not lay aside any of their scientific views regarding the universe. All they are asked to do is to grasp the underlying principles of the copulation of Creation. "SUMMUM is Mind; the universe is mental, held in the Mind of SUMMUM." They will find that the Principles of Summum will fit into their scientific knowledge, and will serve to bring out obscure points and to throw light in dark corners. This is not to be wondered at when you realize the influence of the Summum thought on the early philosophies of Greece, upon whose foundation the theories of modern science largely rest. The acceptance of the Summum Principle of Psychokinesis is the only great point of difference between modern science and the Summum philosophy, and science is gradually moving toward the Summum position in its search for the origins of Crea-

tion. Witness the evolution in physics of the Big Bang Theory.

19   The purpose of this chapter is to impress upon you the
fact that, for all intents and purposes, the universe and its
laws and its phenomena are just as REAL, so far as humans are concerned, as they would be under the hypothesis of Materialism or as held by science today. Under any
hypothesis, the universe in its exoteric aspect is changing,
ever flowing and transitory — and therefore devoid of
substantiality and reality. For anything that is in the state
of change cannot be an absolute. Yet under and of the
same hypothesis, you are compelled to ACT AND LIVE as
if the fleeting things were real and substantial. Under the
old view, mental power was ignored as a natural force,
while under Psychokinesis, it becomes the Greatest Natural Force. This one difference revolutionizes life for those
who understand the principle and its resulting laws and
practice.

20   Take advantage of Psychokinesis and learn to know, use,
and apply the laws resulting from it. Do not yield to the
temptation which, as Summum states, overcomes the partially wise and causes them to be hypnotized by the apparent unreality of things. The consequence is that they wan-
der about like people living in a dream, ignoring the practical work and life of humankind, and are forced into an
awakening at last by their falling bruised and bleeding
over the natural laws which they have ignored. Rather,
follow the example of the wise which the same authority
states, "Use Law against laws; the higher against the lower;
and by the Art of Psychokinesis alter that which is undesirable into that which is perfected, and thus prevail." Fol-

lowing the wisdom, avoid partial wisdom (senselessness) which ignores the fact that, "Mastery consists not in abnormal dreams, visions, and fantastic imaginings or living, but in using the higher forces against the lower — escaping the pains of the lower fields by rising to the higher." Remember always that, "Psychokinesis, not presumptuous denial, is the tool of the Master."

21 Do not live in a world of dreams, but in a universe which, while relative, is real so far as your life and actions are concerned. Your business in the universe is not to deny its existence, but to LIVE, using the laws to rise from lower to higher — living on, doing the best that you can under the circumstances. Rise each day and live, so far as is possible, your highest ideas and ideals. The meaning of life is not known to humans on this level. But the highest few and your own intuitions teach you that you will make no mistake in living up to the best that is in you. Realize the universal tendency is in the same direction in spite of apparent evidences to the contrary. You are all on your proper path, and the road leads ever upward with frequent resting places.

22 Read the message of Summum and follow the example of "the wise." Avoid the mistake of "the partially wise" who digress by reason of their indiscretion.

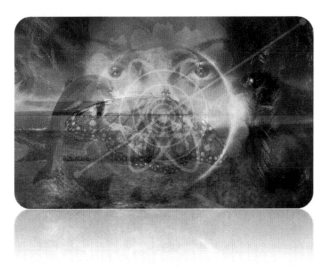

What's the difference between a personal cause and a real cause, a big cause? There is this thing called the "Big Cause." What's the Big Cause? Isn't it Creation itself? The cause of Creation? The thing that makes everything happen? Does the cause of Creation identify itself just with itself, or is it everything? It's everything. So do you think there is a difference between a personal cause and the cause of Creation?

— AMEN RA

CHAPTER 9

SUMMUM in Everything

1   "While everything is in SUMMUM, it is equally factual that SUMMUM is in everything. Those who understand this maxim have great knowledge." — Summum

2   How often have the majority of people repeatedly heard statements that their deity (called by many names) is within everything — "All in all," "God is everywhere," "SUMMUM is in everything." How little have they suspected the esoteric truth concealed by these words? The commonly used expression is a survival of an ancient maxim quoted above. In this statement is concealed one of the greatest philosophical, scientific, and religious truths.

3   You have been given the teaching regarding the mental nature of the universe; the fact that "the universe is mental, held in the Mind of SUMMUM." As stated above, "Everything is in SUMMUM." Note also the corollary statement, "It is equally true that SUMMUM is in everything." This

apparently contradictory statement is reconcilable under the Law of Paradox. It is an exact statement of the relations existing between SUMMUM and Its mental universe. You have seen how "Everything is in SUMMUM." Now examine the other aspect of the subject.

4   SUMMUM is immanent in (remaining within; inherent; abiding within) Its universe, and in every part, particle, unit, or combination within the universe. This statement is usually illustrated by the reference to the Principle of Correspondence. Form a mental image of something — a person, an idea, something having a mental form. A classic example is that of the author or dramatist forming an idea of their characters; or a painter or sculptor forming an image of an ideal that they wish to express through art. In each case you will find that while the image has its existence and being solely within the artist's mind, the author, dramatist, painter, or sculptor is, in a sense, immanent in, remaining within, or abiding within the mental image also. In other words, the entire virtue, life, and spirit of reality in the mental image is derived from the "immanent mind" of the one who expresses it. Consider this for a moment until the idea is understood.

5   As an illustration, let's say that Othello, Hamlet, or Lear existed in the mind of Shakespeare at the time of their conception or creation. Yet Shakespeare also existed within each of these characters, giving them their vitality, spirit, and action. Whose is the spirit of the characters that you know as Micawber, Oliver Twist, Uriah Heep? Is it Dickens or have each of these characters a personal spirit independent of their creator? Do the artworks of Medici, the Sistine Madonna, or the Apollo Belvedere have spirit and

reality of their own, or do they represent the spiritual and mental power of their creators? The Law of Paradox explains that both propositions are true. Micawber is both Micawber and yet Dickens. While Micawber may be said to be Dickens, Dickens is not identical with Micawber. Humans, like Micawber, may exclaim, "The spirit of my creator is inherent within me, yet I am not IT!" How different is this from the shocking partial truth so vociferously proclaimed by many of the partially wise who fill the air with their harsh cries of, "I am God!" Imagine poor Micawber or the sneaky Uriah Heep crying, "I am Dickens"; or some of the characters in one of Shakespeare's plays grandiloquently announcing that, "I am Shakespeare!"

6   SUMMUM is within the earthworm, but the worm is far from being SUMMUM. Still the wonder remains that though the earthworm exists merely as a lowly thing, created and having its being solely within the Mind of SUMMUM, SUMMUM is immanent in the earthworm and in the particles that go to make up the earthworm. Even down to the smallest units discovered by science today, SUMMUM is immanent within them. Can there be any greater mystery than this, of "Everything in SUMMUM; and SUMMUM in everything?"

7   You will realize that the illustrations given above are imperfect and inadequate, for they represent the creation of mental images in finite minds, while the universe is a creation of Infinite Mind. The difference between the two opposing points separates them. Yet it is merely a matter of degree. The same principle is in operation. The Principle of Correspondence manifests in each. "As above, so below; as below, so above."

8   In the degree that humans realize the existence of the indwelling spirit immanent within their being, by directing their ATTENTION to the spirit within and storing potential within that spirit, they empower themselves with the essence of SUMMUM. As they convert their treasure of kinetic mental action to spiritual potential, so will they progress in the spiritual levels of life. This is what spiritual progression means — the recognition, realization, and manifestation of the spirit within you. Regarding this last definition, that of spiritual progression, it contains the veracity of genuine religion.

9   There are many levels of being, many sub levels of life, many degrees of existence in the universe. All depend upon the advancement of beings in the scale, in which the lowest point is the grossest matter and the highest is separated only by the thinnest division from the SPIRIT of SUMMUM. Upward and onward along this scale of life everything moves. All are on the path whose end is SUMMUM. All progress is a returning home. Despite all seemingly contradictory appearances, all movement is toward spiritual development. Such is the message of the Summa Individuals.

10   The Summum teachings concerning the process of the mental creation of the universe are that at the beginning of the creative cycle, SUMMUM in Its aspect of "Being," projects Its Will towards Its aspect of "Becoming," and the process of Creation begins. The process consists of the lowering of vibration until a very low degree of vibratory energy is reached, the point at which the grossest possible form of matter manifests. This process is called the stage of involution, in which SUMMUM becomes "involved" or

"wrapped up" in Its creation. This process has a correspondence to the mental process of an artist, writer, or in-
ventor who becomes so wrapped up in their creation as to
almost forget their own existence and who, for the time
being, almost live in their creation. If instead of "wrapped"
you use the word "rapt," perhaps you will get a better idea
of what is meant.

11   This involutionary stage of Creation is sometimes called
the "Outpouring" of the Divine Energy, just as the evolutionary stage is called the "Indrawing." The extreme opposing point of the creative process is considered to be the furthest removed from SUMMUM, while the beginning of the
evolutionary stage is regarded as the beginning of the return swing of the pendulum of Rhythm. It is the "coming
home" idea held in all of the Summum teachings.

12   During the outpouring, the vibrations become lower and
lower until finally the urge ceases, and the return swing
begins. There is this difference. In the outpouring the creative forces manifest compactly and as a whole. But from
the beginning of the evolutionary or indrawing stage,
there is manifested the Law of Individualization, that is,
the tendency to separate into units of force. Eventually,
that which left SUMMUM as unindividualized energy re-
turns to its source as countless highly developed collective
units of life, having risen higher and higher in the scale by
means of physical, mental, and spiritual evolution. The
individualized units of life join together in harmony, oneness, and communion as they collectively return to their
source.

13   The word "Meditation" is used in describing the process
of the mental creation of the universe in the Mind of

SUMMUM. The word "Contemplation" is also frequently employed. But the idea intended seems to be that of the employment of the Divine Attention. "Attention" is a word derived from the Latin root meaning "to reach out; to stretch out." So the act of attention is really a mental reaching out or extension of mental energy. Thus the underlying idea is readily understood when you examine the real meaning of "Attention."

14   The teachings of the process of evolution are that SUM-MUM, having meditated upon the beginning of the Creation, having thus established the material foundations of the universe and having mentally formed it into existence, awakens or rouses from Its meditation. In so doing, It starts into manifestation the process of evolution on the material, mental, and spiritual levels, successively and in order. Thus the upward movement begins, and all begins to move spiritward. Matter becomes less gross. The units spring into being. The combinations begin to form. Life appears and manifests in higher and higher forms. Mind becomes more and more in evidence. The vibrations are constantly becoming higher. In short, the entire process of evolution, in all of its phases, begins and proceeds according to the established laws of the indrawing process. All of this occupies aeons upon aeons of human time, each aeon containing countless billions of years. Yet the Summa Individuals inform us that the entire creation, including involution and evolution of a universe, is but "the twinkle of the eye" to SUMMUM. At the end of countless cycles of aeons of time, SUMMUM withdraws Its attention — Its contemplation and meditation — of the universe. For the Great Work is finished and everything is withdrawn into

SUMMUM from which it emerged. The spirit of each soul is not annihilated, but is infinitely expanded. The Created and the Creator are merged. Such is the report of the Summa Individuals.

15   The above illustration of the "meditation" and subsequent "awakening from meditation" of SUMMUM is, of course, but an attempt to describe the infinite process by a finite example. Yet "as below, so above." The difference is merely in degree. Just as SUMMUM arouses Itself from the meditation upon the universe, so do humans (in time) cease from manifesting upon the material fields, and withdraw themselves more and more into the indwelling spirit which is "The Divine Ego."

16   There is one more matter I desire to speak of in this chapter. It comes very near to an invasion of the metaphysical field of speculation, although my purpose is merely to show the futility of such speculation. I allude to the question which inevitably comes to the mind of all thinkers who have ventured to seek understanding. The question is, "WHY does SUMMUM create universes?" The question may be asked in different forms, but the above is the gist of the inquiry.

17   Humans have struggled hard to answer this question. Some have imagined that SUMMUM had something to gain by it. But this is absurd, for what could SUMMUM gain that It did not already possess? Others have sought the answer in the idea that SUMMUM wishes something to love; and others that It created for pleasure or amusement; or because It was lonely; or to manifest Its power — all silly explanations and ideas belonging to the childish state of thought.

18   Others have sought to explain the mystery by assuming that SUMMUM found Itself compelled to create by reason of Its own internal nature, Its creative instinct. This idea is in advance of the others. SUMMUM does create and manifest, and seems to find some kind of satisfaction in so doing. It is difficult to escape the conclusion that in some infinite degree It must have what would correspond to the "inner nature" or "creative instinct" in humans, with correspondingly infinite amounts of Desire and Will. It could not act unless It willed to act; and It would not will to act unless It desired to act; and It would not desire to act unless It obtained some satisfaction thereby. All of these things would belong to an "inner nature" and might be postulated as existing according to the Law of Correspondence. But, still, you prefer to think of SUMMUM as acting entirely FREE from any influence, internal as well as external. That is the problem which lies at the root of this difficulty and the difficulty that lies at the root of the problem.

19   SUMMUM merely IS. So you are compelled to say that "SUMMUM ACTS BECAUSE IT ACTS." The ACT of SUMMUM is the copulation of Creation; the joining together and splitting apart of NOTHING and POSSIBILITY infinite times in a finite moment. At the last, SUMMUM is TOTAL Reason in Itself; total Law in Itself; total Action in Itself; and it may be said truthfully that SUMMUM is Its own Reason; Its own Law; Its own Act. Or still further, that SUMMUM and Its act, as Law, are ONE; all being names for the same thing. The Law of Correspondence reaches only to that aspect of SUMMUM which may be spoken of as "The Aspect of BECOMING." Behind that aspect is "The

Aspect of BEING," in which all laws are lost in LAW; all principles merge into PRINCIPLE; and SUMMUM, PRINCIPLE, and BEING are IDENTICAL, ONE AND THE SAME. Therefore, a metaphysical speculation involved with human emotions on this point is futile. I go into the matter here merely to show that the question is recognized, and also the absurdity of the ordinary answers of metaphysics, philosophy, and theology.

If your mother and father can meet inside of you, then your soul will be born. That's what transcending sex is. When you start transcending sex, that's what happens. It is a higher sex. The law of correspondence applies.

— AMEN RA

Chapter 10

The Levels
of Correspondence

1   "As above, so below; as below, so above." —
Summum

2   The second great Summum principle embodies the
idea that there is a harmony, agreement, and correlation between the many fields (levels) of manifestation, life,
and being. This is so because all that is in the universe emanates from the same source. The same laws, principles,
and characteristics apply to each unit or combination of
units of activity as each manifests its own phenomena in
its own field.

3   Note that as you examine the concept of field, the rate of
vibration expresses the degrees or levels of that field. It is a
well-known fact of modern science that everything is in
motion; everything vibrates; nothing is at rest. From the
highest manifestation to the lowest, everything and all

things vibrate. Not only do they vibrate at different rates of motion but in different directions and in different manners. The degrees of the rate of vibration constitute the degrees of measurement on the scale in the fields. These degrees form levels. The higher the degree of vibrational rate, the higher the level, and the higher the manifestation of life occupying that level.

4   There is no need to create an argument by applying terms and a construct to the fields, levels, and dimensions of the universe. Terms would be artificial and arbitrary, for the fact is that all of the levels are but ascending uncountable degrees of the great scale of life. The lowest point is undifferentiated matter and the highest point is that of spirit. The different levels shade into each other so that no hard and fast division may be made between the phenomena on adjoining levels. The atom of matter, the unit of force, the mind of the human, and the being of the archangel are all but degrees in one scale. All are fundamentally the same, the difference depends solely upon the degree and rate of vibration. All are creations of SUMMUM and have their existence solely within the Infinite Mind of SUMMUM.

5   From the bottom of the scale where gross matter begins, the scale ascends and reaches heights where beings of whom you may speak of as angels, archangels, and demigods reside. On some of these levels dwell those great souls whom you call masters and adepts. Above them come the great hierarchies of the angelic hosts, unthinkable to humankind; and above those come those who may without irreverence be called "The Gods." So high in the scale of being are they that their intelligence and power are

akin to those attributed by the races of humankind in their conceptions of deity. These beings are so beyond even the highest flights of human imagination that the word "Divine" is the only word applicable to them. Many of these beings as well as the angelic host take the greatest interest in the affairs of the universe and PLAY an important part in its destiny. These unseen divinities and angelic helpers extend their influence freely and powerfully in the process of evolution and cosmic progress. Known as the Summa Individuals they have superimposed their knowledge and power upon the world, again and again, all under the Law of SUMMUM, of course. Their occasional intervention and assistance in the affairs of humankind have led to the many legends, beliefs, religions, and traditions of the race, past and present.

6   Yet the highest of these advanced beings exist merely as creations of and in the Mind of SUMMUM. They are subject to the cosmic processes and universal laws. They are still mortal. You may call them "gods" if you like, but still they are but the elder sisters and brothers of the race — the advanced souls who have outstripped you. They have foregone the ecstasy of absorption by SUMMUM in order to assist the race on its upward journey along the path. They belong to the universe and are subject to its conditions. Being mortal, their level is below that of absolute spirit.

7   In summary, according to the Principle of Correspondence which states, "As above, so below; as below, so above," all of the seven great Summum principles are in full operation throughout the universes and the levels contained within them. The Principle of Mental Essence of

course applies to all levels, for all are held in the Mind of SUMMUM. The Principle of Correspondence manifests in everything, for there is a connection, harmony, and agreement between the many levels. The Principle of Vibration manifests on all levels. In fact the very vibratory composition of matter and energy defines its level or field of existence. The Principle of Opposition is also operational throughout the cosmos, the extremes of the opposing points being apparently opposite and contradictory. The Principle of Rhythm can be seen in the movement of phenomena having its ebb and flow, rise and fall, incoming and outgoing. The Principle of Cause and Effect is constant; every effect having its inescapable cause and every cause having its effect. Lastly, the Principle of Gender manifests on each level, operating along the lines of its masculine and feminine aspects.

8   "As above, so below; as below, so above." This axiom embodies one of the great principles of universal phenomena.

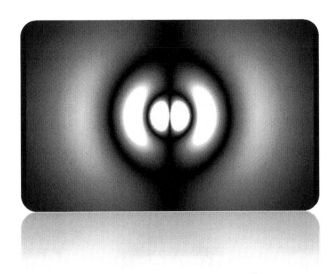

Within Summum, we initially teach a meditation where you receive a word of power. This word has a specific vibration to it, and it resonates inside of you and begins to raise the frequency of the vibration within you. After practicing this meditation for a period of time, you discover that there is indeed something in there. Some people call it self-realization.

— AMEN RA

CHAPTER 11

VIBRATION

1   "Nothing rests; everything moves; everything vibrates." — Summum

2   The great third Summum principle, the Principle of Vibration, embodies the idea that motion is manifest in everything in the universe. Nothing is at rest. Everything moves, vibrates, and cycles.

3   The Summum teachings are that not only is everything in constant movement and vibration, but that the differences between the various manifestations of the universal force are due entirely to the varying rate and mode of vibration. Only SUMMUM, in Itself, vibrates at such a constant rate and with such an infinite degree of intensity that It may be practically considered as at rest. This vibration and movement is generated by the copulation of Creation; "NOTHING and POSSIBILITY come in and out of bond infinite times in a finite moment."

4   Even on the physical level, a rapidly moving object (such as a wheel) seems to be at rest. The Summum teachings are to the effect that spirit is at one end of the scale of vibration, the other end being certain extremely gross forms of matter. Between these two opposing points are billions upon billions of different rates and modes of vibration.

5   Science has proven that all that you call matter and energy are but modes of vibratory motion. Some of the more advanced scientists are rapidly moving toward the position of Summum which holds that the phenomenon of Mind is likewise modes of vibration or motion.

6   Science teaches that all matter can be described in terms of its vibration arising from temperature or heat. Whether an object be cold or hot (both being but degrees of the same scale), it manifests certain heat vibrations, and in that sense is in motion and vibration. From electrons to suns, all particles and objects of matter are in orbital movement; and many of them turn on their axis. The suns move around greater central points, and these are believed to move around still greater, and so on ad infinitum. The molecules of which the particular kinds of matter are composed are in a state of constant vibration and movement around each other and against each other. The molecules are composed of atoms, which, likewise, are in a state of constant movement and vibration. The atoms are composed of little bundles called quanta; electrons, neutrons, quarks, etc., which also are in a state of rapid motion, revolving around each other, manifesting very rapid states and modes of vibration and excitation.

7   Summum teaches that light, heat, and magnetism are but forms of vibratory motion connected with and emanating

from the essence of Creation. A vibratory energy is the cause of the manifestation of cohesion, the principle of molecular attraction and chemical affinity, which is the principle of atomic attraction; and gravitation, which is the principle of attraction by which every particle or mass of matter is bound to every other particle or mass.

8   Creation's Quintessence is the vibratory energy which is the void of space. Summum teaches that this Quintessence is of extreme elasticity and forms universal space, serving as a medium of transmission for waves and particles of vibratory energy such as light and magnetism. The teachings are that the Quintessence is a connecting link between the forms of vibratory energy known as matter on the one hand; and also that it manifests a degree of vibration in rate and mode entirely its own.

9   The hypothetical illustration of a rapidly moving wheel, top, or cylinder shows the effects of increasing rates of vibration. The illustration supposes a wheel, top, or revolving cylinder running at a low rate of speed. This revolving thing will be referred to as the "object." Suppose the slowly moving object may be seen readily, but no sound of its movement reaches your ear. The speed is gradually increased, and in a few moments, its movement becomes so rapid that a deep growl or low note may be heard. Then, as the rate is increased, the note rises one on the musical scale. The motion being still further increased, the next highest note is distinguished. Then, one after another, all the notes of the musical scale sound, rising higher and higher as the motion is increased. Finally, when the motion has reached a certain rate, the final note perceptible to human ears is reached. The shrill, piercing shriek dies away

and silence follows. No sound is heard from the revolving object. The rate of motion is so high that the human ear cannot register the vibrations. Then comes the perception of rising degrees of heat. After a time the eye catches a glimpse of the object becoming a dull, dark, reddish color. As the rate increases, the red becomes brighter. As the speed is increased, the red melts into an orange. The orange melts into a yellow. Then follows successively the shades of green, blue, and violet. Finally, all color disappears, the human eye not able to register them. But there are invisible rays emanating from the revolving object. Electricity and magnetism are emitted when the appropriate rate of vibration is attained.

10   When the object reaches a certain rate of vibration, its molecules disintegrate and resolve themselves into the original elements or atoms. Then the atoms, following the Principle of Vibration, are separated into the countless particles of which they are composed. Finally, even the particles disappear and the object may be said to be composed of the Quintessence. Summum teaches that if the vibration be continually increased, the object would mount up the successive states of manifestation and would in turn manifest the various mental stages; continuing on until it would finally re-enter SUMMUM. The object, however, would have ceased to be an "object" long before the stage of Quintessence was reached. The illustration shows that the destination of constantly increased rates and modes of vibration is spiritward. It must be remembered in the above illustration that at the stages at which the object throws off vibrations of light, heat, etc., it is not actually resolved into those forms of energy (which are much higher on the

scale). It reaches a degree of vibration in which those forms of energy are liberated from the confining influences of its molecules, atoms, and particles as the case may be. These forms of energy, although much higher in the scale than matter, are potentially held in the material combinations by reason that they manifest as material forms. They become entangled and confined in their creations of material forms which, to an extent, is true of all creations — the creating force becomes involved in its creation.

11   The Summum teachings go much further. They teach that all manifestation of thought, emotion, reason, will, desire, or any mental state or condition are accompanied by vibrations; a portion of which are thrown off and which tend to affect the minds of others by "induction." This is the principle which produces the phenomena of psychokinesis, telekinesis, telepathy, mental influence, and other forms of the action and power of mind over mind; all of which the general public is becoming acquainted with owing to the wide dissemination of knowledge by various disciplines.

12   A simple example of vibration and its effects is the influence music has on the mental states of humans. The different rates and modes of vibration within music can take one through the full spectrum of thought, emotion, and mental change. In addition, every thought, emotion, or mental state has its corresponding rate and mode of vibration. By an effort of the Will of the person or of other persons, these mental states may be reproduced just as a musical tone may be reproduced by causing an instrument to vibrate at a certain rate. Likewise, color may be reproduced in the same way. By the knowledge of the Principle

of Vibration as applied to mental phenomena, one may immerse their minds at any degree they wish, thus gaining a perfect control over their mental states, moods, etc. In the same way they may affect the minds of others, producing the desired mental states in them. In short, they may be able to produce on the mental level that which science produces on the physical level, namely, "vibrations at will." This ability, of course, may be acquired only through proper instruction, exercise, and practice in the Summum science known and taught as Psychokinesis.

13   The student within Summum is taught and given the instruction to hear within their minds the mental vibrations and then how to use them. Most advanced and evolved humans can hear within the center of their minds a high pitched frequency or "vibration" known as "Stablematic Feedback," but have never known what it is. With proper instruction, the necessary connections to these mental vibrations can be mastered and used at will.

14   Stablematic Feedback, generated by the bonding and breaking between Nothing and Possibility, is the Sound of Creation. You will find me within this sound. I am in SUMMUM and Summum is in me. Just as it has been said, "I AM THAT I AM," I am that which is in this state of being within the Sound of Creation.

15   A little reflection on what has been presented will show you that the Principle of Vibration underlies the wonderful phenomena of the power manifested by the masters and adepts who are able to apparently set aside the laws of nature. In reality they are simply using one law against another; one principle against others; and accomplish their results by changing the vibration of material objects or

forms of energy. Thus they perform what are commonly called "miracles."

16   As it is said within Summum, "Those who understand the Principle of Vibration hold the scepter of power."

Freedom is only inside of you. It is behind your body, your sexuality, behind your duality, behind your male and femaleness — behind all of those things. Once you can make yourself just one thing, the no thing, when you are the nothing, you are free. If you are something, you are a prisoner of it. Once you become something or anything, then that is your prison. When you are nothing, you are emancipated. It is so simple.

— AMEN RA

CHAPTER 12

OPPOSITION

1 "Everything is dual; everything has an opposing point; everything has its pair of opposites; like and unlike are the same; opposites are identical in nature, but different in degree; extremes bond; all truths are but partial truths; all paradoxes may be reconciled." — Summum

2 The great fourth Summum principle, the Principle of Opposition, embodies the idea that all manifested things have two sides; two aspects; two opposing points; a pair of opposites, with manifold degrees between the two extremes. An understanding of this principle explains the paradoxes which have perplexed the minds of humans. You have always recognized something like this principle and have endeavored to express it by such sayings, maxims, and aphorisms as the following: "Everything is and isn't at the same time"; "every truth is partially false"; "all

truths are a paradox"; "there are two sides to every story"; "there is a reverse side to every coin"; etc.

3   The Summum teachings are that the difference between things seemingly diametrically opposed to each other is merely a matter of degree. It teaches that "the pairs of opposites may be reconciled" and that "thesis and antithesis are identical in nature, only different in degree." The universal reconciliation of opposites is effected by a recognition of this Principle of Opposition. The Summa Individuals claim that illustrations of this principle may be had on every hand, and such illustrations come from an examination of the real nature of anything. They begin by showing that spirit and matter are but two opposing points of the same event, the intermediate fields and levels being merely degrees of vibration. They show that SUMMUM and The Many are the same, the difference being merely a matter of degree of mental manifestation. Thus the LAW and laws are the two opposite points of one phenomenon. Likewise with PRINCIPLE and principles; INFINITE MIND and finite minds. The opposites complement one another, and within all things (events) exists this complementarity. Combined with the various degrees between them, the opposites serve as a complete description of all events.

4   Passing on to the physical level, they illustrate the principle by showing that "hot and cold" are identical in nature, the difference being merely a matter of degree. The thermometer shows many degrees of temperature, the lowest point being called cold and the highest, hot. Between these two opposing points are many degrees of hot or cold. Call them either and you are equally correct. The

higher of two degrees is always warmer while the lower is always colder. There is no place on the thermometer where hot ceases and cold begins. It is all a matter of higher or lower vibrations. The very terms "high and low," which you are compelled to use, are but opposing points of the same event. The terms are relative. So is it with "east and west." Travel around the world in an eastward direction and you reach a point which is called west from your starting point. You return from that westward point. Travel far enough north and you will find yourself traveling south, or vice versa.

5 So is it at the mental level. "Love and hate" are generally regarded as being events diametrically opposed to each other, entirely different, unreconcilable. But as you apply the Principle of Opposition, you find that there is no such thing as absolute love or absolute hate, as distinguished from each other. The two are merely terms applied to the two opposing points of the same event. Beginning at any point of the scale you find more love or less hate as you ascend the scale and more hate or less love as you descend. This is true no matter from what point, high or low, you may start. There are degrees of love and hate, and there is a middle point where "like and dislike" become so faint that it is difficult to distinguish between them. "Courage and fear" come under the same rule. The pairs of opposites exist everywhere. Where you find one phenomenon you find its opposite.

6 It is this fact that empowers the enlightened to alter one mental state into another, along the lines of immersion. Things belonging to different classes of events cannot be altered into each other, but things of the same class may be

changed, that is, may have their vibration changed. Thus love never becomes east or west or red or violet. But it may and often does turn into hate. Likewise, hate may be transformed into love by changing its vibration. Courage may be altered into fear, and vice versa. Hard things may be rendered soft. Dull things become sharp. Hot becomes cold. The alteration is always between events of the same kind but different degree.

7   Take the case of a fearful person. By raising the mental vibrations along the line of fear and courage, that person can be filled with the highest degree of courage and fearlessness. Likewise, the lazy person may change into an active, energetic individual simply by immersion along the line of the desired quality.

8   The student who is unfamiliar with the processes by which the various disciplines of mental science produce changes in the mental states of those around them may not readily understand the principle underlying these changes. But once the Principle of Opposition is understood, it can be observed that the mental changes are occasioned by a change of position on the scale (a sliding along the same scale). The change is not in the direction of altering one thing into something entirely different, but a change of degree within the same thing or emotion, a vastly important difference. Borrowing an analogy from the physical level, it is impossible to change hot into sharpness or loudness into highness, etc. But hot may readily be altered into cold simply by lowering the vibrations. In the same way hate and love are mutually alterable. So are fear and courage. Fear cannot be altered into love, nor can courage be changed into hate. The mental states belong to innumera-

ble classes, each class having its opposite points. It is between those opposite points that alteration is possible.

9   The student will readily recognize that in the mental states as well as in the phenomena of physical fields, the two opposing points may be classified as positive and negative, respectively. Therefore love is positive to hate; courage to fear; activity to non-activity, etc. It will also be noticed that even to those unfamiliar with the Principle of Vibration, the positive point seems to be of a higher degree than the negative, and readily dominates it. The tendency of nature is in the direction of the dominant activity of the positive point.

10   In addition to the changing of the vibration of your own mental states through the operation of the Art of Immersion, this principle may be extended so as to embrace the phenomenon of the influence of one mind over that of another. When it is understood that Psychokinetic Induction is possible, that is, mental states may be produced by "induction" from others, then you can readily see how a certain rate of vibration or alteration of a certain mental state may be communicated to another person and their vibration in that class of mental state thus changed. It is along this principle that the results of many of the mental treatments are obtained. For instance, a person is sad, melancholy, and full of fear. A mental scientist brings their own mind up to the desired vibration by their trained will and, obtaining the desired alteration in their own case, produces a similar mental state in the other by psychokinetic induction. The result is the vibrations are raised and the person is fixed toward the positive end of the scale instead of toward the negative. Their fear and other negative emo-

tions are altered into courage and similar positive mental states. A little study will show you that these mental changes are nearly all along the lines of immersion. The change is one of degree rather than of kind.

11   A knowledge of the existence of this great Summum principle will enable the student to better understand their own mental states and those of other people. You will see that these states are all matters of degree, and seeing thus you will be able to raise or lower the vibration at will. Being able to change your mental vibration, you become master of your mental states instead of their servant and slave. By your knowledge will you be able to aid your fellow humankind intelligently, and by the appropriate methods change the vibration when the same is desirable. All students are advised to familiarize themselves with the Principle of Opposition, for a correct understanding of the same will throw light on many difficult subjects.

Those things that hold us back from evolution happen to be those things that are out of balance. They cause us to move out of the center of the stream of evolution and become grounded on the edge of the river bank. And when we're grounded on the bank, it is impossible to flow down the center stream of evolution.

— Amen Ra

CHAPTER 13

RHYTHM

1   "Everything flows out and in; everything has its
season; all things rise and fall; the pendulum
swing manifests in everything; the measure of the
swing to the right is the measure of the swing to
the left; rhythm compensates." — Summum

2   The great fifth Summum principle, the Principle of
Rhythm, embodies the idea that in everything there is
manifested the copulation of Creation. There is an in and
out; a measured motion; a to and from movement; an outflow and inflow; a swing forward and backward; a pendulum like movement; a tide like ebb and flow between opposing points manifest on the physical, mental, and spiritual levels. The Principle of Rhythm is closely connected
with the Principle of Opposition described in the preceding chapter. Rhythm manifests between the two opposing
points established by the Principle of Opposition. This
does not mean, however, that the pendulum of Rhythm

swings to the extreme points, for this rarely happens. In fact, it is difficult to establish the extreme opposite point in most cases. The swing is ever toward first one point and then the other.

3   There is always an action and reaction; an advance and a retreat; a rising and a sinking in all the affairs and phenomena of the universe. Suns, worlds, humankind, animals, plants, minerals, forces, energy, mind, matter, and even spirit manifest this principle. The principle is active in the creation and destruction of worlds; in the rise and fall of nations; in the life history of all beings; and finally in the mental states of humanity.

4   The copulation of the Nothing and Possibility, Creation's nature, generates Rhythm. Beginning with the manifestations of spirit — of SUMMUM — it will be noticed that there is ever the outpouring and the indrawing; the "exhale and inhale" of Creation's essence. Universes are created, reach their extreme low point of materiality, and then begin their upward swing. Suns spring into being, and once their height of power is reached, the process of retrogression begins. After aeons they become dead masses of matter, awaiting another impulse to bring their inner energies into activity and to initiate a new solar life cycle. The same is true with all the worlds. They are born, grow and die, only to be reborn. So it is with all things of shape and form. They swing from action to reaction; from birth to death; from activity to inactivity; and then back again. So it is with all living things. They are born, grow and die, and then are reborn. The same goes for all great movements, religions, philosophies, creeds, fashions, governments, nations, and all else — birth, growth, maturity, decadence,

death — and then new birth. The swing of the pendulum is always evident.

5   Night follows day and day night. The pendulum swings from summer to winter and then back again. The atoms, molecules, and all masses of matter swing around the cycle of their nature. There is no such thing as absolute rest or cessation from movement. All movement partakes of Rhythm, and the principle is of universal application. It may be applied to any question or phenomenon of the many levels of life. It may be applied to all phases of life. It may be applied to all phases of human activity. There is always the rhythmic swing from one point to the other. The Universal Pendulum is ever in motion. The Tides of Life flow in and out according to law.

6   The Principle of Rhythm is well understood by science and is considered a universal law as applied to material things. The Summum students carry the principle much further, knowing that its manifestations and influences extend to the mental activities as well. It accounts for the bewildering succession of moods, feelings, and other annoying and perplexing changes that you notice in yourselves. Students may learn to escape some of its effect through the use of Psychokinesis.

7   There are generally two levels so far as mental phenomena are concerned, two general levels of consciousness, the lower and the higher. This understanding enables one to rise to the higher level and thus escape the swing of the rhythmic pendulum which manifests on the lower. In other words, the swing of the pendulum occurs on the subconscious level and the consciousness is not affected. This is called the Law of Neutralization. Its operation consists

in raising your attention from your lower ego to your higher ego, above the vibrations of the subconscious level of mental activity, so that the negative swing of the pendulum is not manifested in consciousness, thereby escaping its effects. It's like rising above a force and letting it pass beneath you. In the ocean you can jump above an incoming wave and let its effect pass underneath you. The Summum Master or advanced student immerse themselves at the desired point by a process akin to "refusing" to participate in the backward swing. They raise themselves to a fixed position and allow the mental pendulum to swing back along the subconscious level. All individuals who have attained any degree of self-mastery do this more or less unconsciously. But the masters do this consciously by the use of their Will. They attain a degree of poise and mental firmness beyond belief of the masses who are swung backward and forward on the mental pendulum of moods and feelings.

8   The importance of this will be appreciated by any thinking person who realizes what creatures of moods, feelings, and emotions the majority of people are; and how little mastery of themselves they possess. If you will stop and consider a moment, you will realize how much these swings of rhythm have affected you in your life — how a period of high enthusiasm has been invariably followed by an opposite feeling and mood of depression. Likewise, your periods of courage have been succeeded by equal moods of fear. So it has ever been with the majority of people. Tides of feelings have ever risen and fallen with them, but they have never suspected the cause or reason of the mental phenomena. An understanding of the workings

of this principle will give you the key to the mastery of these rhythmic swings of feelings. You will come to know yourself better, and avoid being carried away by these inflows and outflows. The Will is superior to the conscious manifestation of this principle, although the principle itself can never be destroyed. You may escape its effects on one level, but the principle operates, nevertheless. The pendulum ever swings, although you may escape being carried along with it.

9   There are other features of the operation of this Principle of Rhythm which need to be discussed. There comes into its operation that which is known as the Law of Compensation. One of the definitions or meanings of the word "compensate" is "to counterbalance," which is the sense in which Summum uses the term. It is this Law of Compensation to which Summum refers when it says, "The measure of the swing to the right is the measure of the swing to the left; rhythm compensates."

10   The Law of Compensation is that the swing in one direction determines the swing in the opposite direction or to the opposing point. The one balances or counterbalances the other. On the physical level, you see many examples of the law. The pendulum of the clock swings a certain distance to the right and then an equal distance to the left. The seasons balance each other in the same way. The tides follow the same law. The same law is manifested in all the phenomena of Rhythm. The pendulum, with a short swing in one direction, has but a short swing in the other; while the long swing to the left invariably means the long swing to the right. This law is constant on the physical level and has reference in the natural laws of physics.

11   Summum teaches that mental states are subject to the same law. The person who enjoys keenly is subject to keen suffering; while those who feel little pain are capable of feeling but little joy. There are temperaments which permit little enjoyment and equally little suffering; while there are others which permit the most intense enjoyment, but also the most intense suffering. The rule is that the capacity for pain and pleasure in each individual is balanced. The Law of Compensation is in full operation here.

12   In consideration of the rhythmic swings between pleasure and pain, Summum teaches that to the degree that one experiences the emotion of pleasure or pain, they will swing as far, proportionately, toward the opposite point of feeling. However, in the case where the pendulum has begun its swing towards pain, by utilizing the Law of Neutralization as previously described, one can escape the pain by rising above the effects of the pendulum as it swings towards that point of feeling. According to the Law of Compensation, you are balancing a degree of pleasure and pain previously experienced either in a present life or in a previous incarnation. This throws a new light on the problem of pain.

13   Summum regards the chain of lives as continuous and as forming a part of the overall life cycle of the individual. In consequence, the rhythmic swing, when understood in this way, would be without meaning unless the fact of reincarnation is admitted. Consider for a moment that energy is neither created nor destroyed, and so it is with the life force energizing the soul.

14   Summum claims that the master or advanced student is able, to a great degree, to escape the swing toward pain by

the process of neutralization before mentioned. By rising on to the higher level of the ego, much of the experience that comes to those residing on the lower level of consciousness is avoided.

15   The Law of Compensation plays an important part in the lives of humankind. It will be noticed that one generally "pays the price" of anything they possess or lack. If they have one thing, they lack another. The balance is struck. No one can "have their cake and eat it too." Every situation has its pleasant and unpleasant sides. The things that one gains are always paid for by the things that one loses. The rich possess much that the poor lack, while the poor often possess things that are beyond the reach of the rich. The millionaire may have the inclination toward exquisite dining, but lacks the appetite to enjoy it. He envies the appetite and digestion of the laborer who lacks the wealth and inclinations of the millionaire, but who receives more pleasure from his plain food. Through life, the Law of Compensation is ever in operation, striving to balance and counterbalance; and always succeeding in time even though several lifetimes may be required for the return swing of the Pendulum of Rhythm.

Everything within nature is a beautiful, grand mathematical design. Everything in nature works in mathematical precision under the law of cause and effect. When we allow ourselves to believe we are exempt from cause and effect, we live in a world of illusion and delusion. The message of cause and effect brings one into the ocean of reality, the reality that we are part of a whole rather than isolated from the whole.

— AMEN RA

CHAPTER 14

CAUSE & EFFECT

1 "Every cause has its effect; every effect has its
cause; everything happens according to Law;
Chance is but a name for Law not recognized;
there are many levels of causation, but nothing
escapes the Law of Destiny." — Summum

2 The great sixth Summum principle, the Principle of
Cause and Effect, embodies the idea that law pervades the universe; that nothing happens by chance.
Chance is merely a descriptive term indicating that a cause
exists but is of unknown origin or not perceived. All phenomena is continuous, without break or exception.

3 The Principle of Cause and Effect underlies all scientific
thought, ancient and modern. While many and varied dis-
putes between the many disciplines have since arisen, they
have been principally about the details of the operations of
the principle and sometimes about the meaning of certain
words. The underlying Principle of Cause and Effect has

been accepted as correct by all scientists and metaphysicians. To believe otherwise would be to take the phenomena of the universe from the domain of law and order and relegate it to the control of the imaginary, a circumstance which humans call "chance."

4   A little consideration will prove that there can be no such agent as pure chance. Webster defines the word "chance" as: "the happening of events without apparent cause." In a sense one would be saying that an event is outside of law, beyond the laws of Cause and Effect. How can something act in the phenomenal universe independent of the laws, order, and continuity of the universe? Such a thing would be entirely independent of the universe and therefore superior to it. Yet there is nothing outside of SUMMUM belonging to such a law, because SUMMUM is the LAW in Itself. There is no room for something outside of and independent of law. The existence of such a thing would render all natural laws ineffective and would plunge the universe into chaotic disorder and lawlessness.

5   Careful examination will show that what you call chance is merely an expression relating to obscure causes; causes that you cannot perceive; causes that you cannot understand. The word "chance" is derived from the word meaning "to fall" (as the falling of dice), which approximates the idea that the fall of the dice is merely a happening unrelated to any cause. This is the sense in which the term is generally used. But upon closer examination, it can be determined that there is no chance whatsoever concerned with the fall of the dice. Each time a die falls and displays a certain number, it obeys a law as infallible as that which governs the revolution of the planets around the sun. Behind

the fall of the die are causes or chains of causes extending further than the mind could trace. They may include the position of the die in the hand, the amount of muscular energy exerted in the throw, the condition of the table, etc. All are causes, the effect of which may be perceived. Yet beyond these seen causes are chains of unseen preceding causes, all having a bearing upon the number on the die which comes up.

6   If a die is tossed a great number of times, the count of each number that comes up will turn out to be nearly equal; that is, an equal number of one spots, two spots, three spots, etc. Toss a coin in the air and it may come down either "heads" or "tails." But make a sufficient number of tosses, and the heads and tails will about even up. This is the operation of the law of averages. Both the averages and the single toss come under the Law of Cause and Effect. If you were able to examine the preceding causes, it would be clear that it was simply impossible for the die to fall other than it did under the circumstances and at that time. Given the same causes, the same results will follow. There is always a "cause" and a "because" to every event. Nothing ever happens without a cause or, rather, a chain of causes.

7   Some confusion exists by those considering this principle due to the fact that they are unable to explain how one thing could cause another; that is, how one thing is the creator of a second thing. As a matter of fact, no thing ever causes or creates another thing. Cause and Effect deals only with events. An "event" is "that which comes, arrives, or happens as a result or consequent of some preceding event." No event creates another event, but is merely a

preceding link in the great orderly chain of SUMMUM. The EVENTS are the bonds between cause and effect; the force and energy of Creation. There is continuity between all events precedent, consequent, and subsequent. There is relation existing between everything that has gone before and everything that follows.

8   A stone is dislodged from a mountainside and crashes through the roof of a cabin in the valley below. At first, you may regard this as a chance effect or act of God. But when you examine the matter, you find a great chain of causes behind it. In the first place there was the rain which softened the earth supporting the stone and allowing it to fall. Besides the rain was the influence of sun and wind which gradually chiseled the piece of rock from a larger piece. Then there were the causes which led to the formation of the mountain, its upheaval by convulsions of nature, and so on ad infinitum. Then you might follow the weather patterns which produced the rain, and the materials that the roof was composed of. In short, you would find yourself involved in a mesh of cause and effect from which you would soon strive to disentangle yourself.

9   Just as a human has two parents, and four grandparents, and eight great grandparents, and sixteen great great grandparents, and so on until the number of ancestors run into many millions, so is it with the number of causes behind even the most trifling event or phenomenon. Consider the passage of a tiny speck of soot before your eye. It is not an easy matter to trace the bit of soot back to the early period of the planet's history when it formed a part of a large tree. Follow it from the tree which was converted into coal, to the coal which fueled a fire, to the speck of soot

now passing before your eyes on its way to other adventures. A mighty chain of events, causes and effects brought the speck of soot to its present condition. It is but one of a chain of events which will produce other events continuing on hundreds of years from now; and including the inspiration for this next description.

10   Let us examine the task of rewriting these lines for this day and age. Utilizing a computer and word processing software, we input, format, and store data. We then display the data in a readable form and proofreaders perform their job. The edited copy is sent to a printer to produce printed books and it is also compiled into electronic form. The book is distributed through available channels. You discover the book and buy it. You read it, and it arouses certain thoughts in your mind and that of others reading it; which in turn affects others, and so on, and on, and on. The events continue beyond the ability of humans to calculate further.

11   Just ponder a moment. If a certain man had not met a certain woman in the dim period of the Stone Age, you who are now reading these lines would not be here in the form that you now inhabit. Every thought you think, every act you perform, has its direct and indirect results which fit into the great chain of Cause and Effect.

12   In consideration of Free Will, remember the Law of Paradox. On one hand you do make choices and direct your lives on a conscious level. But the direction of those choices is a result of Cause and Effect, and the partially wise become disillusioned by their refusal of the acceptance of DESTINY. The Summum teachings are that humankind is both free and yet bound by necessity, de-

pending upon the meaning of the terms and the level at which the matter is examined. That is because "the further the creation is from the Center, the more bound it is. As it comes closer to the Center, the more Free it becomes."

13   The majority of humans are more or less slaves of heredity and environment and exhibit very little freedom. They are swayed by the opinions and customs of the exterior world, and also by their own emotions, feelings, moods, etc. They show very little mastery of self. They indignantly protest this assertion saying, "Why, I certainly am free to act and do as I please. I do just what I want to do." They fail to explain where the "want to" and "as I please" come from. What makes them "want" to do this, that, or anything? The Summum Master can change these "pleases" and "wants" into the "Will to will," instead of being moved because some feeling, mood, emotion, or environmental suggestion arouses a tendency or desire within them to do so. They are the masters of their desire, not a slave to their passion.

14   The majority of humans are manipulated by heredity and internal moods, desires, etc. — not to mention outside influences such as the suggestions and will of others stronger than themselves. They are carried along without resistance on their part or the exercise of their will. Moved like pawns on the chessboard of life, they play their parts and are laid aside after the game is over. But the masters, knowing the rules of the game, rise above the level of material life. By placing themselves in touch with the higher powers of their nature, they dominate their own moods, characters, qualities, and vibration as well as the environment surrounding them. Thus, they become movers in the

game instead of pawns; causes instead of effects. The Summum Masters do not escape the causation of the higher levels, but become one with the higher laws. They form a conscious part of the law, rather than being its blind instrument. While they serve on the higher levels, they rule on the material level.

15 On all levels of existence, the law is always in operation and ever in evidence. Look at the phenomenon of the Deep Trance Medium who gives guidance by allowing its body to be used by a disembodied, earthbound spirit. This is due to the cycle of the Law of Cause and Effect. There is the want and desire of the disembodied, earthbound spirit to participate in the embodied game of the material level. There is the want and desire of the medium who is being used to channel other entities, to participate in the game of the spiritual ego.

16 Just as events in life follow the train of cause and effect, so do the events of death. Leverage an understanding of cause and effect as it pertains to your eventual death. Death is a transitory period between this life and the next. It takes you on a path whose direction is determined by the condition of your mind. Your mental state at the time of your death will determine the outcome of events as you make the transition. "As a man thinketh so is he." The last thought you think before you leave your body determines the path you follow to your next life.

17 Normally death leaves you alone in distressed thought, fending for yourself as you begin to move through bewildering surroundings. The familiar territory of your bodily life is gone, your path beset and dictated by fear. But if someone were to preserve your body in such a manner

that it acted as a haven for your essence, and if someone were to provide communication and guidance to your being, the transition stands to be glorious. This is why Mummification and Transference become so vital during this critical movement of the essence. When practiced correctly within the laws of destiny, they set a stage that empowers you to negotiate forces and transition to a life of the greatest realms.

18   The transition that occurs at death is the only time you can really make a momentous change in your destiny. But it is during life that you prepare for the movement. How you fare during your transition is greatly affected by the strength of your Will (or lack thereof). Your Will determines your ability to remain focused on the optimal direction and whether you will be deterred by distractions. Just as there are distractions in life, there are distractions in death. The opportunity to develop your Will is afforded to you in life, when you have the chance to learn and practice meditation. When you can become initiated into the esoteric discipline of an ideal meditation, you have the definitive tool to build the Will of your essence. The strength you acquire in life will play a significant role during death.

19   There is no such thing as chance. Everything is governed by Universal Law. The infinite number of laws are but manifestations of the One Great Law, the LAW which is SUMMUM. It is true that in the Mind of SUMMUM, not a sparrow drops unnoticed. Even the hairs on your head are numbered, just as scriptures have said. There is nothing outside the Law. Nothing happens contrary to it. Yet do not make the mistake of supposing that humankind is but a blind automaton — far from that. The Summum teach-

ings are that humankind may use Law to overcome laws, and that the higher will always prevail against the lower. At last, you will reach the stage in which you seek refuge in the LAW Itself and laugh the phenomenal laws away. Catch this esoteric meaning!

If you were a Neter and you were neutral, you could call down to Earth and say, "Are there any of you down there that have joined your male and your female together and transcended and become nothing, that would like to come bond with us and become something greater as one, and go back to Creation?"

— AMEN RA

CHAPTER 15

GENDER

1   "Gender is in everything; everything has its masculine and feminine principle; Gender manifests on all levels." — Summum

2   The great seventh Summum principle, the Principle of Gender, embodies the idea that there is Gender manifest in everything. The masculine and feminine principles are ever present and active in all phases of phenomena, on each and every level of life. Point your attention to the fact that Gender, in the Summum sense, and Sex in the ordinary accepted use of the term, are similar, but different in scope.

3   The word "gender" is derived from the Latin root meaning "to beget; to procreate; to generate; to create; to produce." Gender is a result of the (copulation) of the TWO Grand Opposites, NOTHING and POSSIBILITY. A moment's consideration will show that the word has a much broader and more general meaning than the term "sex."

Sex refers to the physical distinctions between male and female living organisms. Sex also refers to copulation, intercourse, coitus, and in this context, every EVENT is a form of sex; an IN and OUT relationship between TWO things or opposing points bonding in the same vibrational field (scale).

4 **"Creation manifests when balance is perfected between the opposites. By applying higher Law against lower laws, the Creation becomes divine."**
— Summum

5   This principle of Summum explains that by applying higher Law to what humankind regards as sex, the sexual union can become divine. The sexual union of the physical body and mind, immersed in the vibration of spiritual copulation, will result in the procreation of spiritual offspring. True joy and ecstasy is experienced only in this divine creation.

6   The office of Gender is solely that of creating, producing, generating, etc., and its manifestations are visible on every level of phenomenon. It is somewhat difficult to produce proofs of this along scientific lines, because science has not yet recognized this principle as of universal application. Still, some proofs are forthcoming from scientific sources. There is a distinct promulgation of the Principle of Gender among the subatomic particles such as electrons, the interactions of which form the basis of the chemical bond as your science now knows it. The formation of an ionic compound (such as sodium chloride, common table salt) is caused by the attraction between oppositely charged parti-

cles. That is to say, when sodium gives up a negatively charged electron to chlorine, the sodium becomes positively charged; and when chlorine accepts the electron from sodium, the chlorine becomes negatively charged. The compound, sodium chloride, results because the sodium (+) and chlorine (-) ions are strongly attracted to one another by their opposite charges. Thus, TWO individuals come together and create or generate something that is greater than either one of them could be by themselves. "It takes the joining of TWO to make one — SUMMUM." The most ancient of Summum teachings have always identified the masculine principle of Gender with the positive and the feminine with the so called negative points of electricity — POSSIBILITY and NOTHING.

7   There is a point to be made regarding this identification. The public mind has formed an entirely erroneous impression regarding the qualities of the so called "negative" point of electrified or magnetized matter. The word "positive" has taken on the meaning of something good and strong as compared to "negative" which has the connotation of being bad or weak. Nothing is further from the real facts of electrical phenomena. The so called negative pole of the battery is really the pole in and by which the generation or production of new forms and energies are manifested. There is nothing negative about it. The best scientific authorities now use the word "cathode" in place of "negative." The word cathode comes from the Greek root meaning "descent; the path of generation, etc." From the cathode pole emerges the swarm of electrons. The cathode or negative pole is the mother principle of electrical phenomena. You may substitute the word "feminine" for the

old term negative when speaking of the point of activity. A feminine particle becomes detached from or, rather, leaves a masculine particle and starts on a new career. It actively seeks a union with a masculine particle, being urged by the natural impulse to create new forms of matter or energy (EVENTS). This detachment and uniting, what the chemists term bond making and bond breaking, forms the basis for the greater part of the activities of the chemical world. When the feminine particle unites with a masculine particle, a certain process is begun. The feminine particles vibrate (resonate) rapidly under the influence of the masculine energy, and circle rapidly around the masculine resulting in the birth of a new entity. This new entity is composed of the union of the masculine and feminine (i.e. the positively charged sodium and the negatively charged chlorine). After the union is complete, a new entity emerges and becomes a separate composition (i.e. sodium chloride), having certain properties but no longer manifesting the property of free electricity.

8   The loss and gain of the feminine electrons by atoms is called ionization. These electrons are the most active workers in nature's field. From their unions or combinations arise the varied phenomenon of electricity, attraction, repulsion, chemical affinity (resonance), and the reverse. All this activity originates from the operation of the Principle of Gender on the level of energy.

9   The role of the masculine principle seems to be that of directing a certain inherent energy toward the feminine principle and thus initiating the creative processes. The feminine principle is the one always doing the active creative work — and this is so on all levels. Each principle is

incapable of operative energy without the assistance of the other. In some life forms, the two principles are combined within one organism. For that matter, everything in the organic world manifests both genders. There is always the masculine present in the feminine form and the feminine present in the masculine form. The Summum teachings include much regarding the operation of the two principles of Gender in the production and manifestation of various forms of energy, etc.

10   It is not necessary to recount here the chemical laws of attraction and repulsion between atoms, chemical affinity (resonance), and the attraction or cohesion between molecules. These phenomena are well known and need no extended comment. Take into consideration that all of these laws are manifestations of the Gender principle. In addition, the Summum teachings assert that the very law of gravitation — that attraction by reason of which all particles and bodies of matter in the universe tend toward each other — is but another manifestation of the Principle of Gender which operates in the direction of attracting the masculine to the feminine energies, and vice versa. This cannot be scientifically proven at this time, but examine the phenomena in the light of the Summum teachings on the subject and see if you have not a better working hypothesis than any offered by physical science. Submit all physical phenomena to the test and you will discern the Principle of Gender ever in evidence.

The male force, the masculine gender, is projected into the womb of the pyramid, into the ingredients that make up the nectar. The nectar becomes imbued with a vibratory state that is suspended in time until one ingests it. The body breaks down the nectar and when the alcohol crosses the blood brain barrier, it releases the resonation into your mind.

— AMEN RA

Chapter 16

MENTAL GENDER

1   The students of psychology are well disciplined in the understanding of the subconscious and conscious mind; the voluntary and involuntary mind; the active and passive mind, etc. Even greater understanding has been unveiled with the knowledge of the functions of the left and right brain hemispheres.

2   The Summum doctrine of the Principle of Gender on the mental level has existed throughout the ages. The ancient philosophies took cognizance of the phenomenon of the "dual mind" and accounted for it with the theory of Mental Gender. The concept of Mental Gender may be explained in a few words. The masculine principle of mind corresponds to the left brain; the objective, conscious mind. The feminine principle of mind corresponds to the right brain; the subjective, subconscious mind. Of course the Summum teachings request the student to examine the report of their consciousness by turning their attention inward upon the self. Each student is led to see that their consciousness

gives them first the report of the existence of the self — the report is "I Am." This at first seems to be the final words from the consciousness, but a little further examination discloses the fact that this "I Am" may be separated or split into two distinct parts or aspects which, while working in unison and in conjunction with each other, nevertheless, may be separated in consciousness.

3   While at first there seems to be only an "I" existing, a more careful and closer examination reveals the fact that there exists an "I" and a "Me." These mental twins differ in their characteristics, and an examination of their natures and the phenomena arising from them will throw much light upon many of the problems of mental influence.

4   Begin with a consideration of the "Me," which is usually mistaken for the "I" by the student until the inquiry is pressed a little further back into the recesses of consciousness. People think of self (in its aspect of "Me") as being composed of certain feelings, tastes, likes, dislikes, habits, peculiar ties, characteristics, etc. All of these go to make up their personality or the "self" known to them and others. They know that these emotions and feelings change, are born and die away, and are subject to the Principles of Rhythm and Opposition which take them from one extreme of feeling to another. They also think of the "Me" as containing certain knowledge gathered by their minds and thus forming a part of themselves. This is the supposed "Me" of a human being.

5   The "Me" for most people may be said to consist largely of its identification with the body and physical appetites. Their consciousness is so bound to their bodily nature that this is where they "live." Some go so far as to regard their

personal apparel, cars, and homes as a part of their "Me." These "clothes conscious" people readily lose their personality if divested of their clothing. Even those who are not so closely bound to the idea of personal raiment stick closely to the consciousness of their bodies being their "Me." They cannot conceive of a self independent of the body. To them, their mind seems to be "a something belonging to" their body — which in many cases it certainly is.

6   As humans rise in the scale of consciousness, they are able to disentangle their "Me" from their bodies, and are able to think of their bodies as "belonging to" the mental part of themselves. Even then, they are very prone to identify the "Me" entirely with the mental states, feelings, and emotions existing within themselves. They are very likely to consider these internal states as identical with themselves, rather than "states" produced by some part of their mentality and existing within themselves — of themselves, and in themselves, but still not "themselves." They see that they may change these internal states of feelings by an effort of Will, and in the same way produce a feeling or state of exactly the opposite nature. Yet they notice the same "Me" exists. After a while they are able to set aside these various mental states, emotions, feelings, habits, qualities, characteristics, and other personal mental belongings. They are able to set them aside in the "not me" collection of curiosities and encumbrances as well as valuable possessions. Just as one would shed their clothes, these obstacles can be set aside. This requires much mental Will and power of mental analysis on the part of the student. This undressing of various mental states requires esoteric instruc-

tion found in the teachings of Summum. Still, the task is possible for the advanced student, and even those not so far advanced are able to see, in the imagination, how the process may be performed.

7   Following this laying aside (undressing) process, students will find themselves in conscious possession of a SELF which may be considered in its "I" and "Me" dual aspects. The "Me" will be felt to be something mental in which thoughts, ideas, emotions, feelings, and other mental states may be produced. It may be considered a mental womb, capable of generating mental offspring. It reports to the consciousness as a "Me," with latent powers of creation and generation of mental progeny of all sorts and kinds. Its powers of creative energy are felt to be enormous. It seems to be conscious that it must receive some form of energy from either its "I" companion or else from some other "I" that it is capable of bringing into being through its mental creations. This combined consciousness brings with it a realization of an enormous capacity for mental work and creative ability.

8   The student soon discovers that this is not all that they find within their inner consciousness. They find that there exists a mental something which is able to will that the "Me" act along certain creative lines; able to stand aside and witness the mental creation. This part of themselves they are taught to call their "I." They are able to rest in its consciousness at will. They find there is not a consciousness of an ability to generate and actively create, in the sense of the gradual process attendant upon mental operation, but rather, a sense and consciousness of an ability to project an energy from the "I" to the "Me" — a process of

"willing" that the mental creation begin and proceed. They also find that the "I" is able to stand aside and witness the operations of the "Me's" mental creation and generation. There is this dual aspect in the mind of every human being. The "I" represents the masculine principle of Mental Gender. The "Me" represents the feminine principle. The "I" represents the aspect of being; the "Me," the aspect of becoming. You will notice that the Principle of Correspondence operates on this personal level just as it does upon the grand levels of universal creation. The two are similar in kind, although vastly different in degree. "As above, so below; as below, so above."

9   These aspects of mind — the masculine and feminine principles — the "I" and the "Me" — considered in connection with well known mental and psychic phenomena, turn the master key to those dimly known regions of mental operation and manifestation. The principle of Mental Gender establishes the groundwork for the whole field of the phenomenon of mental influence.

10   The tendency of the feminine principle is always in the direction of receiving impressions, while the tendency of the masculine principle is always in the direction of giving out or expressing. The feminine principle has a much more varied field of operation than has the masculine. The feminine principle conducts the work of generating new thoughts, concepts, and ideas including the work of the imagination. The masculine principle contents itself with the work of the Will in its varied phases. Yet without the active aid of the Will, the feminine principle is apt to rest content with generating mental images received from the outside, instead of producing original mental creations.

11   Human beings who can give continued ATTENTION and thought to a subject use both of the mental principles — the feminine in the work of active mental generation, and the masculine will in stimulating and energizing the creative portion of the mind. The majority of people really use the masculine principle but little, and are content to live according to the thoughts and ideas instilled into the "Me" from the "I" of other minds. It is not the purpose of this work to dwell upon this phase of the subject. Any current psychology text will include a discussion of right and left brain function. Be sure to add to this discussion the key regarding Mental Gender.

12   The student of psychic phenomena is aware of the variations classified under the titles of telekinesis, telepathy, psychokinesis, thought transference, mental influence, suggestion, hypnotism, etc. Many have sought for an explanation for these varied phenomena using the theories of the various "dual mind" teachers. In a measure they are correct, for there is clearly a manifestation of two distinct phases of mental activity. If such students will consider dual minds in the light of the Summum teachings regarding Vibration and Mental Gender, they will see that the key long sought for is at hand.

13   In the phenomenon of telepathy it is seen how the vibratory energy of the masculine principle is projected toward the feminine principle of another person. The latter then takes the seed thought and allows it to develop into maturity. Suggestion and hypnotism operate in the same way. The masculine principle of the person giving the suggestion directs a stream of vibratory energy or will power toward the feminine principle of another person.

The other person accepts it, makes it their own, and acts and thinks accordingly. An idea thus lodged in the mind of another person grows and develops, and in time is regarded as the actual mental offspring of his or her own. In reality, it is like the cuckoo egg placed in the sparrow's nest where it destroys the just offspring and makes itself at home. The normal method is for the masculine and feminine principle in a person's mind to coordinate and act harmoniously in conjunction with each other. Unfortunately, the masculine principle in the average person is too lazy to act, the display of will power too weak. The consequence is that such persons are ruled almost entirely by the minds and wills of other persons whom they allow to do their thinking and willing for them. How few original thoughts or original actions are performed by the average human. Are not the majority of people mere shadows and echoes of others who possess stronger wills than they? The trouble is that the average person dwells almost altogether in his or her "Me" consciousness and does not realize that he or she has such a thing as an "I." They are immersed in the feminine principle of mind, and the masculine principle, in which is lodged the Will, is allowed to remain inactive and not employed.

14 The strong individuals of this world invariably manifest the masculine principle of Will and their strength depends materially upon this fact. Instead of living upon the impressions made upon their minds by others, they dominate their own minds by their Will, obtaining the kind of mental images desired, and moreover dominate the minds of others in the same manner. Look at the strong people; how they manage to implant their seed thoughts in the minds

of the masses, thus causing them to think thoughts in accordance with their highly developed will. This is why the masses of people are such sheep-like creatures, never originating an idea of their own or using their own powers of mental activity.

15   The manifestation of Mental Gender may be noticed all around you in everyday life. There are the magnetic persons, politicians, and movie stars who are able to use the masculine principle in the way of impressing their ideas upon others. The actors and actresses who make people weep or cry as they will are using this principle. So is the successful orator, statesman, preacher, writer, and other people who are before the public attention. The peculiar influence exerted by some people over others is due to the manifestation of Mental Gender, along the vibrational lines described above. In this principle lies the secret of personal magnetism, personal influence, fascination, and attraction, as well as the phenomena grouped under the general classification of hypnotism.

16   The students who have familiarized themselves with psychic phenomena will have discovered the importance of that force which psychology has called "suggestion" — by which term is meant the process or method whereby an idea is transferred to or "impressed upon" the mind of another, causing the second mind to act in accordance therewith. A correct understanding of suggestion is necessary in order to intelligently comprehend the varied psychic phenomena which it underlies. In addition, a knowledge of Vibration and Mental Gender is necessary for the student of suggestion, for they form the basis of the principle.

17   It is customary for those who write about and teach the subject of suggestion to explain that it is the objective or voluntary mind which creates the mental impression upon the subjective or involuntary mind. However, they do not describe the process or give any analogy in nature whereby you may more readily understand the idea. If you will think of the matter in the light of the Summum teachings, you will be able to see that the energizing of the feminine principle by the vibratory energy of the masculine principle is in accordance with the universal laws of nature. The natural world affords countless analogies whereby the principle may be understood. The Summum teachings show that the very creation of the universe follows the same law, and that in all creative manifestations, upon the levels of the spiritual, the mental, and the physical, there is always in operation this Principle of Gender — this manifestation of the masculine and the feminine principle. "As above, so below; as below, so above." Once the Principle of Mental Gender is understood, the varied phenomena of psychology can be intelligently classified and studied, instead of being viewed as an occult subject barred from scientific investigation. The Gender principle "works" in practice because it is based upon the immutable universal laws of life.

18   Further, there is in this present time as there has been in ancient times, an opening of the veil from "above to below" of the masculine force projecting itself into creation. Within the feminine womb of ancient pyramids, masculine vibratory energies were projected by half-god half-human individuals in order to generate living knowledge. This living knowledge was stored as a vibratory state within

liquids known as elixirs, soma, and "Nectars of the Gods." Today, this soma is known as Nectar Publications. The psychokinetic technology of altering the vibratory state of a liquid to hold this masculine energy is an art of the highest mastery. It is the true meaning of TRANSUBSTANTI-ATION, for ordinary ingredients are transmuted to hold the spirit of God.

19   Throughout the ages, the word "spirits" referred to liquids containing ethanol. Since ancient times, only the highest masters were capable of altering these liquids into storage vessels of living knowledge. These masters operate in harmony with higher laws of nature, so that they may rule on the lower levels of manifestation. The minds of those who consume the Nectar Publications are immersed in the living
knowledge. Masculine vibrations are released within the minds of those fortunate students who use the liquids, and they plant the seeds of understanding Creation. No suggestion is required for the vibrations to attune the mind, for they are literally baptized with the knowledge.

20   The application of Mental Gender through the practice of meditation using these sacred publications of creation, constitutes one of the earliest forms of religious worship; a form that scattered itself throughout history and extends itself into our modern times. The spirit of your ancestors resides within the sacred soma. It carries the knowledge of

Creation and awaits to enter you. These vessels of sacred religious worship will open your consciousness to mysteries you will never understand, until you allow them to abide within your spirit, mind, and body.

21 Many books, many of them quite good, have been written on the subject of Mental Gender. The main facts stated in these various books are correct, although the several writers have attempted to explain the phenomenon by various pet theories of their own. By using the theory of Mental Gender, the student will be able to bring order to the chaos of conflicting theory and teachings, and readily make oneself a master of the subject if so inclined. The consideration of the teachings of Summum may clear away many perplexing difficulties — a key that will unlock many doors. It is not necessary to go into detail regarding all of the many features of psychic phenomena and mental science. This material can be easily obtained by the student. With the aid of the Summum teachings, one may go through any library anew. This is not a new philosophy, but rather the outlines of a great world teaching which will make clear the teachings of others — serving as a Great Reconciler of differing theories and opposing doctrines.

Unification is God. God is unification... Then how do you get to unification? You have to have something happen in between. It starts with an S. That is the formula. Devotion equals surrender, and surrender equals unification which equals God. That is the formula.

Devotion = Surrender = Unification = God

— AMEN RA

CHAPTER 17

MEDITATION

1   "Where your ATTENTION is, is where you are."
   — Summum

2   This great Summum axiom embodies the idea that all things are subject to the Principles of Summum, including your ATTENTION and your SPIRIT.

3   Meditation is the process of awakening you to your spirit. Most humankind simply talk about having a spirit, and some believe they have one, but are not really sure. For you are so "involved" in the drama of your physical life that your consciousness is bound up in your ego, and bodily nature and appetites, making you asleep to your spirit. The experience of awakening to the spirit is similar to one most of you reading this book have had. You can call on the Summum principle, "As above, so below; as below, so above," to assist you in your understanding of the experience and how it relates to the search for spirit.

4   Remember those times you were asleep when you realized that you were sleeping, "involved" in dreaming? All at once you realized you were dreaming and that your attention was in your dream. Yet you were able to move your attention to the edge of your dream, next to being awake. There at the edge, next to awake, you decided to go back into your dream and to direct it with your Will in order to fulfill some desire. In other words, you discovered that you could manipulate your dream to some extent by directing it with your Will and attention. Many of you were able to fly in your dreams. You could peer out of your dream and realize you were just dreaming and draw strength from this awareness, with the greater potential of your awakened consciousness. This recognition, while asleep, that you are "just dreaming," and that the real you is on the other side of, or just "as above" sleep, corresponds to the awakening to your spirit.

5   When you discover your spirit, you will be able to draw strength from it in a manner similar to the way you do from the awakened consciousness of your dream state. The conscious realization of your spirit is attained by meditation. As you direct your attention "by meditation" to your spirit and withdraw it from the involvement in the vivid dream of your ego and physical life and bodily appetites, you begin to comprehend how asleep you are. When, through meditation, you awaken to your spirit, you will perceive how humorous you have been to not have known your spirit sooner. Humorous, because being awake to your spirit is so much more awake than graphic physical body life, much the same by comparison as physical body

life consciousness is to your dream in sleep. "As above, so below; as below, so above."

6   As you awaken to your spirit, you begin to realize your eternal nature, and as you realize your eternal nature, your fear of death diminishes. A new perspective of death starts to emerge and you begin to approach the subject with an entirely different attitude. It's an attitude of wonder, curiosity, and learning. The revealing light of life starts to shine because it is when you are no longer afraid of death that you can truly begin to live.

7   **"Against his will he dies, the one that has not learned to die. Learn to die and you shall learn to live, for there will be no one who learns to live that has not learned to die."** — Summum

8   Meditation leads you to your spirit. It leads you to death, and death leads you to life. It is a technique, it is a process.

9   The technique of meditation is IMMERSION; the concentrating of your ATTENTION at a single point, using your Will to fix your ATTENTION at that point. In meditation your ATTENTION is immersed, vibrating at a single point. Using your Will, you prevent your ATTENTION from being attracted to the infinite other points or distractions on the scale of consciousness. The paragon point to immerse in is that point of pure, alert, clear, total, undisturbed, and OPEN consciousness — SUMMUM — the point behind "all action and manifested creation" — above your vivid dream of physical body life. Meditation is the vehicle of "surrender" which transports your ATTENTION to the door behind which your spirit resides. There it lies at the

edge, next to awake, awakening from the "involvement" of the intensity of your physical body life. Meditation is the copulation of your ATTENTION going INTO and OUT of the womb of Creation. An explanation of what is meant by the IN and the OUT follows.

10   **The IN:** When your ATTENTION is fixed (IMMERSED) at that single point in SUMMUM and your ATTENTION begins to harmonize, sing, dance and vibrate in the presence of SUMMUM. You harmonize with the same resonation as SUMMUM which awakens you to your spirit. Just as a tuning fork will pick up the same resonation when held next to or touched by a MASTER tuning fork already vibrating, you begin to resonate with the vibration of that point on the scale of consciousness at which you immerse yourself. **The OUT:** This mental exercise must be balanced with the dance of rhythmic, physical exercise. Thus, the mind, body, and spirit (the whole person) is brought to the center between the point of "all action and manifested creation" and its opposite, the point of SUMMUM.

11   Human beings are constantly engaged in some form of meditation. They allow their ATTENTION to be drawn from one point to another on the scale of consciousness. Yet most humans have little Will to hold their ATTENTION at a single point for any significant period or duration. The result is felt in the general chaos and schizophrenic condition of the mass mind. However, through exercise of the Will by means of holding your ATTENTION at a single point, your Will builds strength. A stronger Will develops which in turn enlarges the circumference of your consciousness and allows you to hold your ATTENTION longer and exercise more.

12   There are no incorrect forms of meditation. The truth is meditation is meditation and "You become what you meditate upon." In other words, "Where your ATTENTION is, is where you are." Automatically, evolution supplies numerous forms of meditation to fulfill the needs of the myriad stages of progression. All these forms of meditation utilize the kinetic energy created by an EVENT to energize the Will with potential energy. Destiny allows for no mistakes. The meditation practiced consciously or unconsciously by all humans is the correct one for them at their stage of evolution. When you master and are fulfilled with one form of meditation, you automatically flow on to another stage of progression.

13   So as not to avoid the issue of the ideal, complete meditation for those "ready to listen and whose minds are OPEN," several components are now presented which, when assembled and practiced, will place you at the door of your spirit's residence. Inside the door, you will find the sacred meditation of Sexual Ecstasy.

The Components of Summum Meditation

14   **1. Mental Exercise** — The IN — You, the student, energize the ATTENTION with the potential energy stored in the Will, directing and immersing the ATTENTION in the point of SUMMUM which is opposite to "all action and manifested creation" — above the vivid dream of physical body life. The IN is the point wherein your ATTENTION, with a rhythmic, mental dance surrenders to the womb of Creation. There the mind is immersed in the presence of the vibration of SUMMUM, infinitely different from "all

action and manifest creation" — above your appetite for the dream of physical body life.

15 **2. Physical Exercise** — The OUT — The body's respiration and heart rate is accelerated for a time equal in duration to the time your attention was immersed in the vibration of SUMMUM. In order to bring mind, body, and spirit (the whole person) into balance and to move to the point of equilibrium between the point of SUMMUM and "all action and manifested creation," a dynamic, physical, rhythmic dance of exercise is practiced to exhaust the spiritual and physical toxins and impurities from the student. The heart, the seat of the soul, will exhaust the anger, jealousies, and imperfections when a rhythmic dance of dynamic exercise is practiced. The breath, the vent of toxins, will exhaust the impurities from the body and allow a higher spiritual vibration to rest within the mind, body, and spirit. The physical exercise is practiced with utmost intensity, and when completed, exhausts the body in a rhythmic dance of creation's pleasure.

16 **3. Purification** — As evolution continues, the mental, physical, and spiritual vibrations of the human race change. For humankind to continue to evolve, the body's vibration must be allowed to change. "You are what you eat" is a truth. The knowledge of eating comes with the opening of consciousness. It is best to avoid eating those creatures whose lives are taken so that you may eat them. "Cleanliness is next to Godliness" is a truth. Much use of water, both internally and externally, provides a purification element. Sleep is a requirement for mind, spirit, and body. Sunshine (contact with the sun) is necessary. Remember, moderation in all things. Silence of mind and

your surroundings is critical, for you will become very sensitive to chaos.

17   **4. Nectar Publications** — Through Psychokinesis (alchemy), the great advanced Masters take juices, plants, herbs, and other ingredients and transubstantiate them into publications of liquid knowledge. These publications, when used under the guidance of the Master, break down the barriers and dissolve the obstacles between the student and the door to the spirit. They are divine keys to unlock the doors to your spirit. The publications have vibrations (resonations) placed within the quanta particles of their substance which, when consumed by the student, cause the mind, body, and spirit to resonate with these same vibrations. These nectars are a wonder of Transubstantiation and their use is a celebration of creation.

18   **5. Devotion** — Without devotion the student cannot succeed. The student must find dedication to something more important to him or her than their self or "their ego." The student must become a DISCIPLE of a Master. This discipleship must be permanent and last a total life time. To be able to immerse IN the presence of SUMMUM, that point opposite "all action and manifested creation," above physical body life, the disciple must leave behind him or herself. Self (ego) will not immerse in SUMMUM, for the ego is a fixation of memories from the points of "all action and manifested creation" — your prison of bodily nature.

19   A great "Master" teacher once said, "When you lose yourself you find yourself." This is the paradox of the whole matter. The goal of finding your spirit seems very elusive when you do not know what you will find. Although, those disciples in search of the answer to what

Creation is will automatically be guided to this vehicle of meditation. A complete, ideal meditation must include TOTAL devotion, trust, surrender, and Love for a Master more spiritually evolved than your self that you are going to lose. This total devotion, this total surrender, this oneness, and this Love must be a complete union with a presently living Master. For nothing rises higher than its source. Therefore, to continue your progression, you must join with a higher source.

20   When you gain total devotion to a living Master, you will no longer need a Master for you will be one yourself. For only a Master can recognize a true Master. Then you will be devoted to the Cause (Summum). This love is not a passion or compassion but a love so complete, you lose all obstacles and conflicts within your consciousness. A surrender not this complete is neither a oneness nor love, but just a compromise. Continue to practice, continue to read, continue to get ready and prepare. There will be no doubt when you truly surrender to a Master. You will awaken either then or in your next incarnation as a Master.

21   What is a Master? A Master is a presently living BEING, an open door to GOD — one who has allowed the human-kindness within to die and is reborn awakened to GOD. A Master is a being who is totally devoted to the cause of creation (SUMMUM) (GOD). A Master is a portal for SUMMUM (GOD). You will know a real Master when you are in the presence of one, for a real Master can take all thought from your mind and breathe the breath of life into you, filling your soul with GOD. Jesus, Osho, Buddha, Krishna, Mohammed, and thousands of others were all at one time living Masters, portals for GOD. They are now in

union with GOD and no longer do they speak as Jesus, Osho, Buddha, Krishna, Mohammed, or as a Master. They have become GOD. They are at a new beginning of eternal progression and infinite evolution. You have their words, their writings, their thoughts, their pictures, and their statues. There are few Masters that forego the final union with SUMMUM (GOD) in order to work the pathways of spiritual evolution and assist the progression of humankind.

22   What a Master is not. A Master is not a church, a temple, a shrine, a building, an idol, a book, a movie, scriptures, doctrines, principles, covenants, ceremonies, records, or words. A Master is not just a teacher. A Master is a portal, an open door to creation (SUMMUM) (GOD). Until you are "FINISHED" preparing to surrender, continue to read, to chant, to meditate, to channel, to pray, to believe, to worship, to attend church and ceremonies, etc. You will never be able to recognize a Master until you are finished getting ready. It is through the surrender to a Master that you will know a Master for God. For in the act of surrender, you become a Master. You see, it takes one to know one. SUMMUM (GOD) cannot flow through you until you become a portal and an open door. Until you go away and die, until you surrender to a Master and are reborn awakened, you will remain an obstacle closed to the flow of GOD's essence through you. You insist on being miserable, you insist on being blind, you insist on being what you think you are. You protect your ego, you defend your beliefs, you build an armor against SUMMUM and GOD. Until you can listen, open your mind, and be touched by a Master of God, you will never recognize or become an open portal for GOD.

23   The perpetuation of this obstacle seems to lie in the fact that most humans are devoted to their personal ego master. The ego master, which you give power to in moments of unbalance, seizes you, overcomes you, reveals you to yourself, and sometimes, even by surprise, succeeds in making you the king of yourself. Here your attention is held, vibrating with the resonation of your lower ego, leaving no possibility for true devotion.

24   Honesty signals the beginning of your surrender as you start to fall in love with the Master. In your meditations, the silence will begin to awaken you to who you are or who you think you are. Feelings of guilt from being dishonest will ascend to the forefront of your consciousness and you will begin to become afraid. It is judgment day, the day of your self-judgment. You will refuse to look at yourself. You will deny and you will struggle. Let go of the guilt. Move on and leave guilt behind by falling ever deeper in love with the Master. As you fall in love, your love will allow you to see your dishonesty, your cleverness, your cunning, your avoidance of truth. The greater your love, the greater your honesty, culminating with your love turning into devotion.

25   **6. Initiation** — With this ideal form of meditation, initiation is necessary. For the disciples who are about to lose themselves to find their spirit, it must be possible for them to know where to look. Their present consciousness is vibrating with "all action and manifested creation" — bound in the intense dream of physical body life, thus preventing their attention from knowing where to look. The disciple needs to surrender to a Master that is a portal for SUMMUM and vibrates with the resonation of the open

consciousness of SUMMUM. The vibration within the Master is what the disciple is given. This will add light to the mystery, "That the father is in me and I in him."

26   This esoteric initiation is similar to the previously stated analogy of the resonating tuning forks. The disciple (tuning fork) is placed next to the Master (the other tuning fork) who resonates with the vibration of SUMMUM. The Master then instills the resonation within the disciple's soul and the disciple and the Master become one. Thus, the disciple is brought into permanent union with Stablematic Feedback, bonded with "The Sound of Silence," with "The Sound of Creation" Itself. You, the disciple, will find me in the Sound of Creation, and I will guide you to your next destination.

27   This connection is necessary, like a choice culture for yogurt or a prize yeast for fine champagne. You can have all the right ingredients, but without the activation or catalyst, there are no actual results. The yeast is the catalyst for the fermentation process which turns grapes into wine. To quote another example, a tiny piece of metal in the form of a key must be used to turn on the powerful engine of an enormous vehicle. No key — no travel.

28   This initiation cannot be told or read about, but only given through a living Master, by communion (oneness), a union, a physical bonding with the Master. It is an art that cannot be learned through reading, hearing, seeing, or any of the senses. Truly, it is a "Gift" from a god.

29   A collective meditation is most preferred. The effectiveness of the mental exercise is increased by practicing in a group. The mental exercise becomes even more effective when practiced in a group within a Summum pyramid.

Likewise, the results of physical exercise are enhanced when the exercise is practiced in a group as opposed to by yourself. For the sum of the collective group in meditation is greater than the individuals alone.

Obstacles and Barriers

30   Most human minds allow their ATTENTION to be attracted to so many events in thought and action, that they dwell in the field of possibility somewhere near the point of "CLOSED" consciousness. They are involved with the concerns of their personal ego master. They are involved in their physical body life.

31   Excuses are a predominant obstacle to eliminating all obstacles. Excuses are created by your personality (ego) to justify and rationalize its behavior. So long as you excuse yourself, no progression is possible. The process of awakening to your spirit involves knowing your own tendencies, and admitting the real motives behind your actions.

32   Dwelling in action, spiritually asleep in its vivid dream of physical body appetites, near the point of closed consciousness, the human mind modifies its perception of reality through the following:

33   **1. Correct Idea** — Holding a perception of something (a process of mentally "defining" something with which you make contact), or accepting the testimony of a qualified expert regarding something, and judging that perception or point of view to be the "right" or "proper" or "only way" to perceive it.

34   Perception is dependent upon perspective, and perspective is your position in space-time and consciousness.

There are many perspectives for viewing things, whether it be something tangible like a pencil or intangible like a subjective idea. For example, to a person viewing the sun from the Earth, it may appear as a large, yellow ball of intense light. To a person viewing the sun from a planet in the outer reaches of the solar system, it appears as a small, bright, blue star. Another person may view the sun as a dynamic system of fusion between hydrogen atoms. Yet all three points of view, although different, are valid.

35 Be aware of wanting to be "correct" or "right" because the attitude, the arguments and judgments that arise from it, will limit your perception. Humankind has a tendency to turn a point of view into the "right" or "only" way. Even the Summum philosophy can be turned into the "correct" way, but that would destroy it. Take note of your attitude and remember the Divine Paradox. Everything is partially true. Everything is correct and incorrect. The enlightened recognize all perspectives. They have cast aside the judgments which fix humans to single points of view and obstruct progression.

36 **2. Misconception** — Under correct idea, the viewpoints given may be considered rational viewpoints. Misconception is forming an irrational idea regarding an object of perception. For example, a war veteran who has suffered extreme stress during his war experience and has returned to civilian life may view civilians as the "enemy." Misconception entraps the human mind in illusion.

37 **3. Fancy** — Creating a fantasy, an idea for which no corresponding object of perception exists. This occurs when humans, seeking to fulfill a need or desire of their ego, pretend that a certain situation exists when they know

it does not; or imagine that a certain situation exists, but they have no knowledge if it actually does exist. In fancy, the human mind dwells upon the feature of illusion, and ignores the practical work of life and the natural laws of existence. Fancy places one in a state of ignorance to the extent that knowledge can only be gained through direct experience. Keep in mind the systematic law of learning. Until you have eaten an almond, you will never really know what an almond tastes like. Likewise, until you totally surrender to a Master you will never become one.

38   **4. Sleep** — As previously noted in the components of Summum Meditation, sleep is a requirement in that the body, mind, and spirit require rest. However, sleep becomes an obstacle in the sense that when you sleep, you allow your ATTENTION to be with your subconscious mind. When you wake from sleep, your ATTENTION is brought back to your conscious mind. You may feel good, bad, or indifferent about your sleep. The fact that you feel about your sleep indicates that you were still on the points of action. Even when you are physically awake, all your ATTENTION is with your conscious or subconscious which makes you, in effect, asleep rather than awake to your spirit.

39   As you awaken to your spirit through Summum Meditation, you can abide within your spirit while sleeping, RESTING IN THE STATE OF BEING, instead of falling unconscious to your spirit. Just as the cat who sleeps with the abandon of a child, yet whose instinct is ever alert, so too can you remain awake to your spirit even though you sleep.

40   **5. Memory** — HOLDING ON and MENTALLY RECRE-
ATING a correct idea, misconception, fancy, or sleep.

41   MEMORY plays a dominant role in the human mind.
Memory is an accumulation of all the infinite lives you
have lived. The mind is constantly collecting data through
the senses, conscious and subconscious. Nothing escapes
your mind — it is the record of your existence. This collective memory is held not only within your brain but also
within every cell of your body.

42   You are an accumulation of the genetic message from the
egg and sperm of your parents. This is the destiny of your
physical body and mental condition. The union of the
sperm and egg that creates you contains the memories of
the whole evolution of humankind. It holds the collective
mind of all the generations before you. The combination of
your soul and your ego makes you a very complex crea-
ture.

43   The programmed genetic memory of your body is
stronger than that of your mind or your Will. You will notice that every time you try to change the "NATURE" of
your body the body usually wins out. You cannot resist the
NATURE of your body, for it is a compilation of the human race. You alone cannot win a battle against human
nature. Do not battle nature, flow with nature. Sing and
dance with nature. The process of the egg and sperm joining together, the resulting outward growth and activity of
your body (the gastrulation), follows the same stages as
Creation Itself. Your body is a miniature representation of
the whole creation, the whole progression of evolution —
in anthropology this concept is termed "ontogeny recapitu-
lates phylogeny."

44   Do not battle nature. Do not battle your body. When you do, you are trying to defeat all of evolution. Instead, harmonize with your body and with nature. Harmonize in a rhythmic dance with nature and the nature of your evolutionary body. Feel with your body. Listen to your body. The practice of meditation is a battle with the mind, not the body. It is a struggle of your Will to take control over the mind. Meditation is completely sensitive. Your mind is insensitive, and you have allowed the body to become insensitive.

45   Whenever you become angry, it is due to the memories contained within either the mind or body. If the anger comes from a need of the body, it is a bodily memory. If it does not come from a need of the body, it is mind memory. Watch where your anger comes from. Be aware of your anger. If this anger is just a mental habit, then be aware of it. The memory of the mind, of all past actions, is a conditioned thing. Repeating the past, you act just like an automaton.

46   Whenever you allow your mind to accumulate memories, it is because you have no confidence in your present actions. Your mind goes through many rehearsals of many different situations. You have no confidence about acting NATURALLY. You must prepare for your actions, saying them many different ways in your mind. You are caught by chaos in the mind, out of harmony with nature, and in a battle with DESTINY. You have lost your rhythmic dance with nature. This struggle is the torture of human existence.

47   When you fall in love (devotion) you feel it in your body. Every cell of your body falls in love, yet the mind is trying

to rationalize what is happening. It judges, criticizes, condemns, and holds you in chaos. Such a sad state is this confusion of mind against body — it is a separation from nature and harmony.

The Solution

48   **Balance** — Bringing yourself to the point of equilibrium through balance between mind, body, and spirit produces the complete person. By neutralizing the swing of the pendulum, your Will is focused towards the center, between the opposing points of extremes. The mind surrenders through meditation, rhythmically dancing into the music of pure, alert, clear, total, undisturbed, and OPEN consciousness  in the presence of SUMMUM; and the body is brought to sensitivity through dynamic, rhythmic dance — physical, exhaustive exercise.

49   This ideal meditation is the Grand Master Key to Reconciliation and the powers of spiritual psychokinesis. With the reconciliation of the two extremes neutralized and brought into balance, the disciple allows for a smooth, continuous evolution. When the disciple develops the powers of spiritual psychokinesis, he or she becomes a master of the universes. Truly, it is "MAGICAL."

What is in control? Are you in control? Is your inner self in control? Or is everything else around you in control? I'm speaking here of your meditation. The meditation is given to you for a very specific purpose. It is the most important thing that you have ever learned since you were born. There is nothing more important that you've been exposed to. There is nothing more significant that you have been exposed to. The intensity of the practice is very, very important.

— AMEN RA

CHAPTER 18

SUMMUM AXIOMS

1   "The possession of knowledge, unless accompanied by an expression of action, is like the hoarding of precious metals — a vain and foolish thing. Knowledge, like wealth, is intended for use. The Law of Use is universal, and those who violate it suffer by reason of their conflict with natural forces." — Summum

2   The Summum teachings are not intended to be merely stored away and secreted. "If you don't use it you'll lose it." Beware of Mental Miserliness and express into action that which you have learned. Study the axioms, but practice and teach them also. Given below are some of the more important Summum axioms with a few comments added to each. Make these your own and practice and use them, for they are not really yours until you have used and taught them.

3 "Experience is the best teacher." — Summum

4 The Systematic Law of Learning must be applied to all principles in order for one to have real knowledge rather than just belief. This learning requires you to first question the principle. Secondly, you must take activity in the principle and experience the action or the "cause and effect" of the principle. Thirdly, you move to a knowledge about, rather than a belief in the principle, for the principle and its workings become yours through experience.

5 "To change your mood or mental state, change your vibration." — Summum

6 You may change your mental vibrations by an effort of Will, by deliberately fixing the attention upon a more desirable state. Will directs the attention and attention changes your vibration. Cultivate the Art of Attention by means of the Will through meditation, and you have solved the secret of the mastery of moods and mental states.

7 "Strengthen and enlarge the Will by accumulating kinetic energy from the field of 'all action and manifested creation.' Convert the kinetic energy into potential energy and store it in the Will through meditation." — Summum

8 By accumulating kinetic energy and altering it to potential energy for use by the Will, your Will may be strengthened and enlarged. Energize the attention with potential

energy from the Will, then immerse the attention and the Will within SUMMUM. While immersed in SUMMUM, your Will and attention are energized with the very essences of Creation. During this immersion, kinetic energy from the field of all action and manifested creation is altered into potential energy for storage in your Will.

9   "To alter an undesirable rate of mental vibration, put into operation the Principle of Opposition and concentrate upon the opposite point of that which you desire to suppress. Dissolve the undesirable by withdrawing your attention from it." — Summum

10   This is one of the most important of the Summum formulas. It is based on true scientific principles. The mental state and its opposite are merely the two contrasting points on the same scale. By mental immersion the vibration can be altered. This principle is known to modern psychologists who apply it to the breaking up of undesirable habits by instructing their students to concentrate upon the opposing quality. If you are possessed of fear, do not waste time trying to "kill it." Instead, cultivate the quality of courage and the fear will disappear. Some writers have expressed this idea most forcibly by using the illustration of the dark room. You do not clear out darkness. Just open the curtains, let in the light, and the darkness disappears. To dissolve a negative quality, concentrate the attention on the positive point of that same quality. The vibrations will gradually change from negative to positive, until finally you become fixed on the positive point. The reverse is also

true, as many have found to their sorrow when they allowed themselves to vibrate too constantly on the negative point. By changing your vibration, you may master your moods, change your mental states, remake your disposition, and build up character. Much of the mental mastery of the advanced Masters is due to this application of immersion which is one of the more important aspects of mental psychokinesis. Remember the Summum axiom which says:

11   **"Mind (as well as metal and elements) may be altered Psychokinetically, from state to state; degree to degree; proportion to proportion; condition to condition; point to point; vibration to vibration. Psychokinesis is Mental Mastery."**

12   The mastery of immersion is the mastery of the fundamental Principle of Psychokinesis or mental alteration. For unless one acquires the art of altering their own vibration, they will be unable to affect their environment. An understanding of this principle will empower one to change their own vibration as well as that of others, if you will but devote the time, care, study, and meditative techniques necessary to master the art. The principle is true, but the results obtained depend upon the persistent patience and practice of the student.

13   **"Rhythm may be neutralized by an application of the Art of Immersion."** — Summum

14   As explained in a previous chapter, Summum holds that the Principle of Rhythm manifests on the mental levels as well as the physical. Further, the bewildering succession of moods, feelings, emotions, and other mental states are due to the backward and forward swing of the mental pendulum that carries you from one extreme of feeling to another. Summum also teaches that the Law of Neutralization enables one, to a great extent, to overcome the operation of Rhythm. There are both higher and lower levels of consciousness. By rising mentally to the higher level, the Master causes the swing of the mental pendulum to manifest on the lower level, and by dwelling on the higher level, escapes the consciousness of the swing backward. This is effected by immersing in the higher self, and thus raising the mental vibrations of the ego above those of the ordinary levels of consciousness. It is similar to the process of rising above a force and allowing it to pass beneath you. The advanced students immerse themselves at the positive point of their being — the point of spirit — rather than the point of personality. By refusing to participate in the operation of Rhythm, they raise themselves above its level of function. Standing firm in their statement of being, they allow the pendulum to swing back upon the lower levels without changing their fixed position of immersion. This is accomplished by all individuals who have attained any degree of self-mastery, whether they understand the law or not. Such persons simply refuse to allow themselves to be swung back by the pendulum of mood and emotion, and by steadfastly affirming the superiority of spirit, they remain fixed on the positive point. The Masters, of course, attain a far greater degree of proficiency, because they un-

derstand the law which they are overcoming through the use of a higher law. By use of their Will, they attain a degree of poise and mental steadfastness almost impossible to believe by those who allow themselves to be swung backward and forward by the mental pendulum of moods and feelings.

15 Remember always, however, that you do not really destroy the Principle of Rhythm, for that is indestructible. You simply overcome one law by counterbalancing it with another, thus maintaining an equilibrium. The laws of balance and counterbalance are in operation on the mental as well as on the physical levels. An understanding of these laws seemingly enables one to "overthrow" laws, while in fact they are merely exerting a counterbalance.

16 **"Nothing escapes the Principle of Cause and Effect (Destiny), but there are many levels of the law, and one may use laws of the higher to overcome the laws of the lower." — Summum**

17 An understanding of the practice of immersion allows you to rise to a higher level of Cause and Effect and thus counterbalance the laws of the lower levels. By rising above the level of ordinary causes you become, to a degree, a cause instead of an effect. Able to master your own moods and feelings and to neutralize Rhythm, you are able to escape a great part of the operation of Cause and Effect on the ordinary level. The masses are carried along, obedient to their environment. The wills and desires of others overpower them, and the effects of memory and inherited tendencies rule them so that they tend to move about on

the chessboard of life like mere pawns. By rising above these influencing causes, the advanced student seeks a higher level of mental action and direction. Dominating their moods, emotions, impulses, and feelings, they create for themselves new characters, qualities, and powers through which they overcome their environment. They now become the players instead of mere pawns. Such people assist in the game of life, instead of being moved about this way and that by stronger influences, powers, and wills. They use the Principle of Cause and Effect instead of being used by it. Of course, even the highest are subject to the principle as it manifests on the higher levels. But on the lower levels of activity, they are masters instead of slaves. As Summum says:

18   "The wise serve on the higher, but rule on the lower. They obey the laws coming from above them, but on their own level and those below them they rule and give orders. Yet in so doing, they form a part of the Principle instead of opposing it. The wise fall in with the Law, and by understanding its movements operate it instead of being its blind slave. Just as the skilled swimmer turns this way and that way, goes and comes at will rather than being carried like a floating log, so are the wise as compared to the novice. Yet both swimmer and log, wise and fool, are subject to Law. Those who understand this are well on the road to Mastery."

19 **"True Psychokinesis is a Mental Art." — Summum**

20   In the above axiom, Summum teaches that the great work of influencing one's environment is accomplished by mental power. The universe being wholly mental, it follows that it may be ruled only by mentality. In this fact is to be found an explanation of all the phenomena and manifestations of the various mental powers. In back of and underneath the teachings of the various disciplines remains ever constant the principle of the mental substance of the universe. If the universe be mental in its essence, then it follows that mental alteration must change the condition and phenomena of the universe. If the universe is mental, then mind must be the highest power affecting its events. If this be understood then all the so called "miracles" and "wonder workings" are seen plainly for what they are.

21   **"There is no why. It merely is and is not." — Summum**

22   Why does SUMMUM do what It does? Why is there life? Why is there being? These can be difficult questions to answer, and can be dealt with by saying that the questions are their own answers. SUMMUM does for the cause of doing. Life is the reason for life. Being is for the cause of being. Perplexing as it may seem, just know that you can "be" with these concepts, and through practicing the ideal meditation, attain the realization that everything is and is

not, simply because it is and is not — it is the result of Creation's copulation.

23 **"SUMMUM is INFINITE, LIVING MIND. The universe is mental. The Summa Individuals call It SPIRIT!"** — Summum

24 Your new physics, that of quantum mechanics, has proposed startling new theories, so far as the scientific world is concerned, dealing with the behavior of the universe and the nature of reality. Quantum physicists are now faced with the conclusion that "reality" is a product of consciousness. Their study of subatomic particles, or more recently, quanta particles, suggests to them that these particles, as small as they appear, have a consciousness entirely their own. Such being the case at the quantum particle level, it must follow that all matter and energy in the physical universe has its own collective consciousness, since matter and energy are but groupings of these quanta particles. Therefore, the material universe itself has a consciousness all its own. Quantum physicists are faced with the question of the source of the consciousness of matter.

25 As your physicists continue in their search for the source of the consciousness of matter, they will discover that all matter has spirit. This spirit they try to understand as a form of consciousness. The collective spirit of all the units and groupings of units is SUMMUM. It is this collective consciousness which makes up the INFINITE, LIVING MIND which is SUMMUM. SUMMUM is not some sort of "giant brain in the sky," but rather the Life Force energy produced by the event of the bonding between NOTHING

and POSSIBILITY. Just as your consciousness is much more encompassing than the organ that is called your brain, so is the INFINITE, LIVING MIND of SUMMUM that much greater than all the collective raw particles of the universe. SUMMUM is infinite consciousness in all its varied aspects. The Summa Individuals call It SPIRIT!

26 **"Creation manifests when balance is perfected between the opposites. By applying higher Law against lower laws the creation becomes divine."
— Summum**

27 Under and behind all outward appearances or expressions of existence, behind all events, behind all circumstances, is the substantial essence — the bonding between Nothing and Possibility. It is for this reason that the universe is dual in its nature, and it is for this reason that spiritual development requires you to become conscious of that duality. Whenever you examine anything, be aware of the duality of that which you observe. Be aware of the two opposites which make it up to be what it is. Remember, where you find one thing, you will always find its opposite.

28 By recognizing the duality of the universe, you can begin to look for the opposites in all events or circumstances, remembering always that the opposites are merely differing aspects of the same thing or event. In identifying the opposites, you can strive for balance between the two. Your perfection of balance between the opposites is achieved by the practice of the ideal meditation, for this practice will bring you to the point of equilibrium between

body, mind, and spirit. This practice will move you to a perspective that is unencumbered by judgments and the constraints of a fixed mind.

29   As you perfect your balance between the opposites, be ever aware of the correspondence between the levels of life and being. Keep in mind that the same principles are in effect at all the various fields and levels. Utilize the Principle of Correspondence to reason from the known to the unknown and observe the laws as they operate on each level. Apply the law of a higher level against that of a lower level, for the law of a higher level dominates the lower.

30   In perfecting your practice of the ideal meditation and becoming intimate with the Summum principles, you will develop the powers of spiritual psychokinesis. Thus, you are able to easily and more readily use Law against laws, the higher against the lower, and create a life and direction of your choosing. In such a position, you are most certainly in harmony with nature and truly your creations become divine.

Amen

EPILOGUE

"Energy can neither be created nor destroyed. It can only change from one form to another."

Among scientific circles, this is known as both the Law of Conservation of Energy and the First Law of Thermodynamics. Science has concluded through experimentation and observation that the forms of matter and energy within the universe are never created and never destroyed. The total amount of energy in the universe always remains the same, and energy can only transform itself. If we consider this law as of universal application, not only does it apply to grosser forms of energy such as light and matter, it also applies to subtler forms of energy such as mental ideas and the life force inhabiting a human body.

Religions and philosophies for thousands of years have acknowledged the effects of this law in the concept of reincarnation. The essence behind one's existence is subject to this fundamental law. The death of the physical body does not signify a destruction of that essence. Rather, death initiates a change in form. Ancient cultures had a very keen and intimate understanding of the essence and its relationship with the physical body. They were able to manipulate the death process to the point that the changing of states of the essence could occur at a much greater level, allowing themselves to be catapulted forward in the development of their being. This was the reason behind ancient mummification, and the reason why Summum re-introduced mummification to society in a modern, contemporary form.

Some people have held the belief that when you reincarnate, you wake up in your next lifetime having a memory of your prior life. But this cannot happen unless certain things take place and those particular things do not typically occur. A person's essence does not contain memories. Memory is tied to the body for it is a function of the brain. Chemicals stored within the brain correspond to the memories we have. It is these stored, chemical, vibratory patterns that make up our memories. While a person's essence may be affected by the memories, the essence does not contain the memories. Memory is accumulated in the brain. When the body dies and deteriorates, the chemical patterns dissolve and the memory is gone, unless one's body is preserved through mummification. Then memories can be maintained.

The essence does not carry on memory of a previous lifetime. What it carries on is you. The essence accumulates residual vibrations and familiarities that come from experiences. You may find yourself familiar with this or attracted to that, although you do not know why. Just prior to the essence re-incarnating, it hovers around a copulating couple, then gravitates towards the pregnant woman and waits for the baby to be born. Given the advances in science, other opportunities for reincarnation arise. The essence may observe a laboratory and wait for the birth of a test tube baby. At a future time it may linger around a fetus that will be born out of an artificial womb, or it may await the birth of a clone.

In any event, as the baby takes in its first breath of life, the essence enters the body. You receive the evolutionary genetics of your parents held within the DNA that serves as the blueprint for this new body. The genetic memory determines your physical traits and characteristics and greatly defines your personality. Still, your essence contains residual vibrations that continue and go on. Brothers and sisters, born and raised in the same family, sharing the same genetics, exposed to the same environments, find themselves having different interests and attractions.

In 1979, Ron Temu, a dock worker in southern California, began traveling to Summum in Salt Lake City, Utah, to listen to Summum Bonum Amen Ra aka "Corky" Ra give philosophy presentations. These presentations began as a result of encounters Corky had with what he describes as advanced beings. Ron and Corky had been college friends, and when Corky told Ron of his experiences, Ron decided to find out what Corky had to say in his presentations. Up to this point, Ron had been involved in a personal spiritual inquiry for a number of years. He had been investigating and reading, attending workshops and seminars, looking for answers to questions that had developed in his mind. Ron found Corky's presentations so compelling that for years he would travel to Salt Lake on a regular basis and listen to Corky discuss topics such as creation, vibration, rhythm, and others.

Around 1983, Ron came across a book he found at the Bodhi Tree bookstore located on Melrose Avenue in West Hollywood, California. The book was called *The Kybalion*, by Three Initiates. Ron began reading the book at the bookstore and was so enamored by it, he bought it, drove home, and read the entire book that day. The book so charmed and captivated his attention. It addressed questions and tied information together. It complemented and confirmed the information he received at Corky's presentations. Something about it was familiar and personal. Ron told Corky about the book and exclaimed, "Corky, this is what you are talking about! What you've been talking about for all these years is in this book!"

But Ron saw and felt a big difference between *The Kybalion* and Corky's presentations. To Ron, *The Kybalion* was just a book of words. While it had great information that touched him, it was just a book. Corky, on the other hand, would present the concepts in a very unique manner. Corky brought a life to the ideas and could elaborate on them in a way that just can't be found in a book. Corky had never heard of the book and asked Ron to bring it to Salt Lake. Corky, myself, and others read the book and agreed, it was a great little book. It said many of the things Corky had been teaching Ron and others at the classes. It re-affirmed the things Corky had been initiated into during his divine encounters.

The Kybalion was written in the early 1900s by authors who only identified themselves as "Three Initiates," an intriguing title. Why would they not give their names as the authors of the book, yet refer to themselves as Three Initiates? In their humble honesty, they state in the book they cannot take credit for the work, for it only surmises something that has been around for ages. But in that same honesty they identified themselves as Three Initiates. Why would they do that, unless of course, they were actually initiated by someone or something?

Ron attempted to ascertain who the Three Initiates were and who initiated them. He researched the publisher of the book, the Yogi Publication Society, and determined the funding of the publication came from the Masons. Ron began contacting Free Mason groups to get more information about the book, but no one claimed it or seemed to know anything about it. He contacted the Masonic Temple in Chicago, Illinois, where the Yogi Publication Society was apparently located, but it was to no avail. As far as he could determine, an offshoot lodge of the Masons published the book. In comparing other Masonic information with *The Kybalion*, Ron found *The Kybalion* to be significantly different and therefore did not think the Three Initiates went through any type of Masonic initiation. But the information in *The Kybalion* was so compelling that Ron and others would agree the Three Initiates went through some type of divine, initiatory experience.

Sages throughout time have stated when certain ideas are publicly presented, people can become outraged. Religious people seem to be particularly prone to the outrage for they feel it offends their religion. Most people have heard or read stories about individuals in history who claimed divine encounters and then were persecuted or ridiculed. The Three Initiates had a compelling experience. They did not give details for they knew of the anger they would encounter.

History is filled with stories from differing cultures about compelling initiatory encounters with the divine. These stories are accepted by many people. Yet it seems the story can only be acceptable if it is a story about the past. It becomes difficult to accept by people if it is a story about something that occurred in the present day. Had they given details about their initiation, had they discussed further details about the principles and given the whole story about them, the Three Initiates would have infuriated people. They knew this and even went on to make this statement in *The Kybalion*.

Ron's research of *The Kybalion* indicated the principles in it were once part of an ancient rabbinical text that was kept among certain Jewish rabbis. The text disappeared following the Christian Crusades when Christians had burned

books. The story was that Moses of the Old Testament received principles carved on stone tablets after a divine encounter. The principles were too much to understand for
the people at that time and Moses destroyed the tablets.
Moses received a second set of tablets with other principles
more easily understood by the infantile people he was to
lead. But Moses revealed the original principles to certain
individuals who were capable of understanding and acting
upon them. The principles were handed down by word of
mouth amongst rabbis who later wrote them down only to
become lost after the crusades.

While the principles cannot truly be lost since they make
up the fabric of existence, writings about them can be.
Over time, many books have indirectly referred to them,
but as a whole, the principles became diluted and distorted. Three individuals re-introduced the principles in an
unadulterated form following an initiation back in the late
1800s, early 1900s. They wrote things down, progression

continued, and today, there are people who meet in a pyramid for in-depth discussion about these concepts.

Still, many people read about the principles, but don't do anything about it. They read and discuss and talk and read, but nothing happens with them. As the Three Initiates stated, you need to apply the principles in your life, use them, experience them, become part of them in order to make them real and truly understand them. So Corky started teaching about the principles at Summum after he was initiated into them by the advanced beings, the Summa Individuals, beings who are complete and whole. This is how Corky first found out about the principles. Then Ron introduced *The Kybalion*. Now when Corky looks back in life, he says there is a familiarity with things about *The Kybalion* that he did not realize until a certain point in his life. Ron had a familiarity possibly with people who had brought about the original publication of *The Kybalion*.

At this point I should state *The Kybalion* makes a very significant omission. It does not contain the one Grand Principle from which all the other principles come. Perhaps this was on purpose. Perhaps it was too much for the people of the time to understand and the Three Initiates elected not to divulge it. But today there are a few people who can grasp it for it was introduced to Corky during his initiation, and Corky introduced it to me and others who have been through initiations given at Summum. Today, there are some individuals who are attracted to this principle. There are people who have considered the idea in some fashion, even though it was never formally introduced to them. The Principle of Creation is the binding or birthing principle for the other principles of *The Kybalion* and Summum. They would not be without the Principle of Creation. While the principle may appear very abstract at first, when one becomes involved in serious study about it, the principle begins to reveal itself.

And so, when Corky was preparing to write a book about the Summum philosophy, he decided to use *The Kybalion* as an outline since this is essentially what *The Kybalion* discussed. *The Kybalion* had fallen into the public domain and under laws of the land Corky could create a derivative work from it. By adding the Grand Principle of Creation to it, by discussing additional details about the principles along with further concepts, and by rewriting content in a style and language more appropriate for today's modern era, *The Kybalion* has evolved into *SUMMUM: Sealed Except to the Open Mind*. As *The Kybalion* states, all things change. The Principles of Creation are once again presented in a pure, complete, and contemporary manner.

To truly understand these principles, you need to use them in your life. You will be attracted to these principles as your essence becomes more and more familiar with their workings. Some people are already attracted to them because of work they have done in this or previous lifetimes. Others are not for their work has yet to begin. Those of you who feel no affinity to these principles may first need to search and develop yourselves in other ways. But in the end, you will reach a point where you begin to study them and become initiated into them.

There are people who after discovering Summum, traveled hundreds even thousands of miles to visit in Salt Lake. Something touched them and they felt compelled to come. For some, it signaled the start of something new. For others, it was picking up where they last left off. Either way, it becomes a time when the mysteries and wonder of the universe beckon, and nature invites you to dance with creation.

Summum Bonum Anu Aua

ABOUT THE AUTHOR

Summum Bonum Amen Ra aka Corky Ra was born November 2, 1944, in Salt Lake City, Utah. He was an infectious, playful, and charismatic person who also happened to be an ordinary guy. At birth, he was given the name Claude Rex Nowell. His parents divorced in 1948 and he moved with his mother to southern California  where she remarried to Robert Williamson King. Claude's mother had his name legally changed to Claude Rex King, but he always had the nickname of "Corky," and that was how he was known to family, friends, and many others.

From 1948 to 1959, Corky lived in the foothills of Monrovia, California, in an area called Oak Glade Park. Then his parents moved to Tustin, California, where Corky graduated from Tustin High School in 1962. He attended Orange Coast College in Costa Mesa, California, and graduated in construction technology. In 1964, Corky moved back to Salt Lake City where his father lived and legally changed his name back to Claude Rex Nowell. He attended Brigham Young University and the University of Utah, got married, raised two children, and was divorced.

In 1975, Corky experienced what he said was an encounter with highly advanced beings who introduced him to the underlying forces of nature. That same year, he founded Summum, a 501(c)(3) non-profit organization for the purpose of sharing with others the "gift" he received from his angelic teachers. He began teaching philosophy classes on a number of topics that included meditation, the cause of Creation, and seven fundamental principles. A few years later, he established Summum as Utah's first federally bonded winery in order to create the Nectar Publications for use in meditation. In 1980, Corky legally changed his name to Summum Bonum Amon Ra as a reflection of his spiritual path, and generally went by Corky Ra.

Corky passed away January 29, 2008, and was the first person to undergo Summum's practice of Modern Mummification and Transference. His body is sealed inside a gold, bronze Mummiform where it will rest for all time and eternity. He is the world's first modern mummy, and even in death, Summum Bonum Amen Ra continues to touch people with his transcendent legacy.

For Continued Study...

Summum publishes a companion study guide to *SUM-MUM: Sealed Except to the Open Mind*. The study guide contains exercises that, when completed, will give you a better understanding of the Summum philosophy. The study guide is available through the Summum website at:

www.Summum.us

Summum offers video recordings of classes given by Summum Bonum Amen Ra. To watch them, visit:

www.Summum.tv

Audio class recordings are also available for listening at:

www.kphi.org

For Further Reading...

Sexual Ecstasy from Ancient Wisdom
by Summum Bonum Amen Ra

Ancient Egyptian hiero-
glyphs reveal a wealth of
knowledge regarding human
sexuality. This work is a trans-
lation of the ancient hieroglyphs and uncovers hidden
mysteries once known only to
those ancient ones. Egyptian
meditative sexual practices are
explained so that the methods
and techniques can be understood and applied today.

Filled with beautiful illustrations, this educational and
instructional book contains treasured information for both
men and women. Following its guide and direction will
bring you joys not felt for thousands of years. Regardless
of your age, this book can educate you into a state of pro-
longed sexual ecstasy. For more information, visit:

www.SexualEcstasy.org

Made in the USA
Las Vegas, NV
17 November 2021